Interim Management

Interim Management

The new career choice for senior managers

Second edition – completely revised

Dennis Russell
and
Ian Daniell

AVETON BOOKS

Aveton Books
The Eyrie
Sandhills Road
Salcombe, TQ8 8JP
England

Interim Management was first published in 1998 by Butterworth-Heinemann.
This second edition, completely revised, published 2005 by Aveton Books.

British Library Cataloguing in Publication Data

A catalogue record for this book is obtainable from the British Library.

ISBN 0-9549742-1-2

Typeset bt TW Typeseting, Plymouth, Devon
Printed by TJ International Ltd, Padstow, Cornwall

The cover photo is from the Hotel Sojka – Slovenia.

Contents

Foreword to the First Edition

by Sir Leonard Peach

Sir Leonard Peach, MA (Hons.) Oxford was Group Director of Personnel for IBM, Chief Executive and Personnel Director of the National Health Service Management Board, President of the Institute of Personnel Management, Commissioner for Public Appointments, (advising on departmental procedure for ministerial appointments), and also Chairman of the Policy Studies Institute, and Chairman of the University of Westminster.

I spent thirty of my forty years in management with IBM – one of whose practices was 'full employment'. This, translated, meant a commitment to job security providing that the employee was willing to agree to being retrained and redeployed if necessary, though there was always a recognition that such a practice could only be fulfilled if the business was sustained by an economy functioning at an appropriately supportive level. The effect of this commitment and other employee-centred principles was a stability of labour force in an industry that frequently suffered skill shortages and heavy loss rates. The labour turnover of IBM United Kingdom in the period from 1975 to 1990 rarely exceeded 3%. Self-sufficiency and labour stability were ways of life.

Then it all changed. The problems which beset IBM in the early 90's resulted in substantial reductions in the labour force, on a voluntary and generous basis. As part of the incentive to leave the company, IBM United Kingdom set up a separate company. Those who 'took the package' had the right to be registered with that organisation, to be re-employed on a part time basis by IBM, (which like so many other companies made reductions which were too severe in some functions), and also to be offered to other employers on a part time or full time basis at a price. It was a great success and the company quickly built up a substantial turnover and profitability. Since I was Chairman, I was able to see its impact on many of those who had lived in what some would argue was the 'cocooned' existence of IBM. Many of them blossomed, became 'short term managers', professionals and consultants with other organisations. This was my first contact with 'Interim Management' and both the customers and the contractors seemed very happy with the result. Indeed, it was impressive to see the entrepreneurial and business instincts which were released by the new found freedom.

One good result from the recessions of the early 80s and the early 90s was the recognition that many able people became available on the labour market, whose employment history did not show the stability which was a characteristic and perhaps a requirement of an earlier period. This has also convinced some employers that they too may gain from individuals with width and variety of experience, rather than depth in one particular company or industry and that, in given situations, the injection of talent and competence for a short term may be more productive than reliance on individuals with long continuous spells of employment. There has been a corresponding increase in the growth of Interim Management.

This period coincided with the growth in popularity of Professor Charles Handy's work. His name is frequently mentioned in the text and he is the management guru mostly associated with the growth of portfolio management in its various forms. The concept of part-time work, part-time service to the community, and part-time education and leisure as a way of life has grown in popularity and provided a supply of recruits ready to fulfil Interim responsibilities. It is worthwhile spending a few lines on self-development, an important facet of the portfolio approach.

I returned to IBM just a few days ago and heard how an experiment in the recruiting of graduates which had begun in the late 80s was progressing. This was initially a pilot scheme where new graduates were recruited on a contract of four years with a limited benefit provision and a lump sum payment at the end of the contracted period. It is now widespread within IBM United Kingdom Ltd, recognised by graduates as providing an excellent training in the Information Technology industry, and the company itself is satisfied with the flexibility in the labour force which such schemes provide. I heard much about the high morale and commitment of this group, but, I commented to my informant, 'As long as they're in charge.' In other words, if the graduate's skills continue to be upgraded, if they feel they have a ready market and can freely exercise their choice to put themselves on that market with the conviction that they can find new opportunities, then morale is high.

The same must apply to those who pursue Interim Management or professional careers at a later stage in life than the graduates whom I was describing. They must have confidence in themselves and their abilities, they must continue to upgrade their competencies and their skills, they must develop their analytical and diagnostic skills recognising that every situation has unique elements, and the solution for the current customer is not necessarily the same as that which they employed in a previous situation. There are still too many consultants or managers with solutions in search of a problem. The writers of this book are well aware that Interim Management is not for everyone, and of the importance of Continuing Professional Development in ensuring employability on a short-term or long-term basis. Much of the material is contributed by practising Interim managers who set out the advantages and disadvantages of choosing this form of career and provide sensible advice based on their own careers.

My own experience indicated that Interim Management is an important addition to the approaches which can be used to take an organisation through a period of instability when the previous leadership has failed; where it needs a new dimension to compensate for the weaknesses of the current management; or to add value in a specific field where the organisation is inexperienced. A brief injection of new thinking and energy may provide the incentive, relief or quality of thinking which provide energy, stimulus or accelerated results which all organisations require from time to time. I commend this book to those bodies seeking such a solution, and to those individuals who feel that this way of making a living will provide the challenges which other forms of employment have failed to do.

Authors' Preface to the Second Edition

Dennis Russell writes: Serendipity is lovely, when it happens. And there was certainly an large slice of it lying in wait for me when I started work on a Second Edition of 'Interim Management'. Almost the first thing I did was to approach the Interim Management Association for some guidance on the current state of the market, (I thought that a lot might have changed since I retired, just when the book was originally published in 1998. How right I was!) The first person I spoke to was Ian Daniell, then coming towards the end of a successful three-year stint as Chairman of the IMA. His instant reaction was, 'We should meet.' So began our collaboration, over lunch in the bar at the Institute of Directors. The serendipity was that Ian had decided to go for a Professional Doctorate based on his work in Interim Management, and wanted to find a way of getting his work published, while I obviously needed the benefit of his current experience and research. So we became a true partnership. Of course a lot of the basics of the first edition still hold true – even that happy insight that 'the average daily rate for an Interim assignment is about 1% of the appropriate salary for the job'. But a lot has changed too – particularly in the direction of Interim Management becoming a professional career of choice, with new entrants tending to be younger than before. As I feared, the State – especially the taxman -has become much more aggressive in seeking to corral independent workers into tighter regimes. I owe a debt to everyone who has contributed to either or both editions, and I would like to especially thank John Webster, of The Chief Executives Office Ltd., whose work still features largely in Chapters 4 and 5 and Appendix VI.

I found, from reading the life stories of the newer breed, (see Appendix II) that my favourite quotation is still a good battle-hymn for the aspiring Interim:

> *Out of the night that covers me*
> *Black as the pit from pole to pole*
> *I thank whatever Gods may be*
> *For my unconquerable soul.*
> (William Henley)

Ian Daniell writes: I undertook to start my Doctorate in 1999, and the following year was talked into taking over as the Chairman of the Interim Management Association. This was a very busy and challenging time, as we re-branded, re-launched and re-structured the Association, and of course I was still running my own Service Provider company.

With a Professional Doctorate, (unlike a PhD), I am given credit for the contribution I have made to the profession. I leave others to judge what that was, but suffice it to say that by 2003, when I handed over as Chairman, all that remained to be done for my Doctorate was my final project, of which this book will be part.

The collaboration with Dennis has been a rewarding experience, and the delays we have encountered have been entirely of my making. His original work was the first authoritative book on Interim Management to be published in this country, and the second edition has been a real challenge. As I worked on it I was made to realise the areas in which we still had a lot to find out about the Interim Management business.

For example, we still have no generally accepted idea as to the size of the market; we have only a vague idea of the way external factors impinge on the market for Interim Management; and we have only a very general understanding of what makes a good Interim.

I am delighted to have been appointed Industry Champion by the IMA, and hope to be able to come up with some answers to these questions, and more, over the next few years. In the meantime I am confident that this second edition will be accepted as a worthy successor to Dennis' first edition, and will be of value to potential Interims and clients alike.

Faversham, June 2005

Part One

The Business of Interim Management

1 *What is the Interim Management story?*

A definition

Let's start by stating *what Interim Management is not.* It is not working temporarily at one job while you are waiting for your next 'proper job' to come along. That is a perfectly sensible and respectable thing to be doing, of course, and many people do it. Perhaps it could reasonably be labelled 'temporary management', but it is NOT what this book is about.

By 'Interim Manager' we mean a person who has made a career choice to be an *independent portfolio worker*. '*Portfolio*' because, instead of employment with one organisation, he generates his income from a portfolio of activities – a consultancy analysis for this company, a training course to be written and delivered for another, and of course an interim (i.e. temporary or locum) management role for a third. Sometimes all three at the same time! What he does, for the purposes of this book, is less important than the *terms* under which he does it. Most commonly he is the *independent* owner of his own business, which *charges him out by the day*, under a contract to deliver a certain result. Senior medical consultants and barristers are familiar to us as professionals who traditionally function in this INDEPENDENT way. Actors – and window cleaners – are quite similar. If you go back a few hundred years, most workers with a skill were self-employed, hence the rise of the great guilds that were their associations. 'Interim Managers' are new additions therefore to a long and honourable list. Here's a quick example of what they can do:

A SAFE PAIR OF HANDS

A major plc had a subsidiary which manufactured electronic components, mainly for the motor industry. Its management had failed, and there was a looming shortfall in sales which threatened its very survival. No one in the parent group with the necessary competence was keen to take it on, for fear of getting sucked down with it. An experienced Interim Manager was introduced. Over a period of 9 months he shaved costs, rationalised professionally, renewed the focus on customer satisfaction and service, identified new products and new markets, achieving a strong turnaround into profit. He then helped with the selection of a permanent manager from within the group, and mentored him in for a successful handover.

How did we get here?

By 'here' I mean at the point where this new role of Interim Manager is recognised, by most larger companies at least, as not just a way of filling a gap but also as a useful addition to the human resource strategies available for controlling costs and achieving objectives.

I think there are three key contributors to this success story:

- **Supply**
- **Demand**
- **Professional Provision**

Supply became abundance about 30 years ago when that great economic disaster, the oil crises of the 1970s, hit the world's industry like a tidal wave. Huge increases in the price of the principal fuel of our civilisation forced nearly every business to bring forward the (probably long overdue) review of the cost of employing their staff. Up to then companies maintained a kind of folk memory of post-war shortages of skilled people, and hoarded staff 'in case we need them'. Now it became necessary to throw overboard *any* weight that was not essential lest the whole boat go down! First industrial workers, then industrial managers, then service workers and service managers – no section of the economy escaped the knife – though perhaps 'axe' is the better metaphor, because over the years the butchery has been done with a less than perfect vision of the future needs of the business or relative qualities of the individuals concerned. Denationalisations and the subsequent slimming down of bloated former monopolies had a marked impact. Takeovers and mergers had a special effect, because often the people 'let go' were the managers of the losing companies – irrespective of quality. Especially the awkward, able, *dangerous* people. Over recent years there has been a new breed of recruits into Interim Management, slightly younger than before, people with the resources to be financially and psychologically independent, who have *deliberately chosen* the self-employed way of life.

Demand follows as the logical consequence of supply! The pressure to hold down costs is continuous and insistent. But the shedding of experienced staff itself produces gaps in the corporate skill-base, which are only exacerbated when the company finds itself moving onto unfamiliar ground. So when a strategic need or a gap arises, it may well suit a company better to find a skilled Interim Manager, rather than try to shuffle around or extend already highly stretched corporate executives. Because there is a wide range available of people *who can prove they have 'done it before'*, companies can take in an Interim Manager with real confidence of getting a good result.

Professional Provision is the result of the coming together of two complementary effects: firstly, a rapid realisation by Interim Managers and users of Interim Managers alike that the ones who were *committed* to the lifestyle performed very much better, to the point that *only* full-time committed professionals get the worthwhile assignments. Secondly, over the last 10 years, there has been a rapid corresponding growth of **Interim Management Service Providers** – agencies who specialise in finding the best Interim Managers on behalf of client companies, and who have an important role in helping companies define the assignment more precisely, so that the ideal choice of candidates can be put forward. In turn their professionalism is being sharpened by the development of their trade body, the **Interim Management Association**.

This book is about helping *individuals* to decide if independence is the right career move, and about helping *corporate managements* decide when and how to use an Interim Manager.

Summary of Chapter 1 – What is the Interim Management story?

1. Interim Management is a new full time profession for independent portfolio workers – not a 'between jobs' activity.
2. The rationalisations of the last 30 years have created both the need for Interim Managers and the resource from which they can be drawn. More recently, younger people are confidently choosing to 'go independent.'
3. The full time commitment of Interim Managers combines with the professionalism of the IM Service Providers to raise standards and improve results.

2 The changing nature of Interim Management

Good, so you have got this far. Let's hope that you are not just idly flicking through this in the bookstall of an airport lounge or whilst waiting for the Eurostar but have actually decided to invest in your future and to read through the whole book. In this chapter we want to talk about how Interim Management has changed over the past decade and dispel a few of the myths. More importantly we want to suggest to you that IM is a sensible career and lifestyle option which *might* suit you, if not now then sometime in the future.

Some history

There is no getting away from it, even if you had heard of Interim Management 10 to 15 years ago, your view was likely to be fairly jaundiced. It was seen as the last resort of the redundant executive trying desperately to squeeze a few more years out of a job market that was increasingly competitive, selective and ageist. Perhaps you might remember seeing a job advert for an engineering director who must be a graduate, chartered engineer, several years of general management experience and still be under 35! There didn't seem time to fit it all in but that seemed to be what the market wanted.

Those putting themselves forward as potential interims in the early 1990's were predominantly male, white, over 55 and financially secure as a result of one of those hefty redundancy or early retirement packages which were so popular at that time. Their skill sets covered most job functions and industry sectors with a bias towards general management, finance and accounting and production with a strong weighting towards Manufacturing which was being forced into a decline in the UK. The Interim Service Providers (agencies) were a very mixed group: there were some who were highly professional and effective, and there were others who were primarily ordinary recruitment agencies intent on jumping on this new bandwagon. Whilst the Association of Temporary Interim and Executive Services, ATIES, (now the IMA) was doing its best to introduce some degree of conformity, and reliable standards, there was still on long way to go, (and incidentally there still is). The consequence of all this was that potential clients considered Interim Management to be at best a means of managing a gap and at worst a last ditch attempt to stave off an imminent crisis.

So what has changed?

Interim Management is all about people. Without people prepared to work as freelances there can be no service. So the rest of this chapter will focus on how the raw material of the industry, people like you perhaps, has changed. We are not ignoring other forces like the market, the perceptions and generally favourable experience of client companies or the widening expertise of the Service Providers. All of these are considered later, but for now the focus is on the individual and how their age, motivation, aspirations and skill sets have changed since the early 1990's. The hope is that this will reinforce our contention that Interim Management is a realistic, worthy and rewarding professional undertaking and one which can be considered as a viable career option. *We strongly recommend that you try to put some flesh on the necessarily bare bones of this chapter by reading Appendix II, which features the personally-written stories of a number of practising Interim Managers.*

1. Age

Let's first address the age issue. In many ways this is where it started. When companies and major organisations had to cut costs, most did it by down-sizing. Of course it wasn't usually put as bluntly as that. Heaps of consultants were called in to pronounce wisely about the merits of business process re-engineering, de-layering, flattening management structures, widening the span of command or whatever the management fad was that week. It would be sadly cynical to suggest that all of these were merely cost cutting exercises, but in many cases the casualties were the expensive, experienced senior managers who were approaching an age when, it seemed, they had reached their ceiling. They could be replaced by younger and therefore cheaper managers, and would be paid off largely out of the surplusses in the pension funds, swollen by the inflation which had contributed to the problem in the first place. This of course then meant that many of those 'let go' would inevitably turn to Interim Management or 'consultancy' for the rest of their working lives.

But now of course we have an interesting paradox. Although many of the corporate casualties were senior executives and managers, there was also a notion that age and seniority could be equated with experience and success. That the grey hairs had been hard won over many years on the corporate battlefields suggested maturity and gravitas. The younger managers and executives who had survived the successive boardroom culls lacked that experience and so Interim Managers could be called in to give some of it back again. However Interim Management is not just about experience. It is about results. It is about achievement and it is about success. The notion that age and experience alone will lead to the desired end-result is not valid. Interim managers must of course be experienced but they must also have a demonstrable track record of success and achievement and that need not come with age. If you want someone who has successfully started and sold on a dotcom company it is unlikely to be a 50 year old. It is much more likely to be someone who doesn't wear a tie, may not own a suit and hasn't yet reached 40!

All of that is a way of saying that the average age of people starting as Interim Managers has come down. There is anecdotal evidence, backed up by research and surveys, to support this and whilst the average age of a practicing IM is now in the mid to late 40s, the average age on starting as a freelance is 5 years less than that. Now given that there are still a lot of 50 plus managers who are operating in this way that actually means that some active IMs will be in their 30s. There is still discussion in the industry as to whether someone that young can actually have the relevant experience and track record to be a true Interim Manager but let's leave that alone for the while and look at why they should want to do it in the first place.

2. Motivation

Motivation is always a fascinating subject, to me at least. Why do people do what they do and when they do it? What is the trigger which is going to make someone respond or behave in a particular way? The importance of this to the practising interim is discussed later on when we consider the art of negotiation but for now I want to consider why executives and senior managers are being attracted to a career as Interim Managers.

Having interviewed literally thousands of Interim Managers over a good number of years I have come up with *6 main reasons* why individuals go down this path. Having said that, they are not discrete and tend to merge in together, but broadly speaking they are (not necessarily in order of importance):

Challenge and Variety

Desire to use one's skill to achieve positive and specific results; Need to earn; Dissatisfaction with corporate life, and a Strong urge to redress the work/life balance.

Professionalism

The over-riding desire of so many of those looking at Interim Management for the first time is to do a good job. They want to use the skillset gained over many years to achieve results, unencumbered by corporate politics and the associated baggage. Hardly surprisingly, most Interim Managers have a strong results focus which gives them considerable job satisfaction. This 'high protein' approach to work is very challenging and given the variety that an independent career implies, it can also be very rewarding both professionally and materially.

Corporate Life

Dissatisfaction with corporate life does not just end with the politics. Our working lives have changed. 'Jobs for life', if ever such a thing truly existed outside the public sector or major corporations, are long gone. The unwritten psychological contract which so many employees, even at a senior level, felt they had with their company or organisation has been broken for ever. The paternalistic notion of career progression and job security has been replaced by a much less structured concept of 'employability'. Instead of keeping an individual in the corporate cocoon throughout the working life, employers can make it easier to discard their workforce by giving them transferable skills so that they can be moved on with a relatively clear conscience. Interim Management is sometimes not the first choice of the redundant executive, *but it is redundancy that often forces individuals to reflect on what they really want out of life.*

Work/life balance

It is not hard to imagine a model of corporate life similar to Charlie Chaplin's huge machine that devours our time and energy in pursuit of impersonal goals such as 'share-holder value' and 'return on investment'. Lives are fed daily to the machine, sucked dry of effort, energy and enthusiasm leaving only emptied husks to return home at the end of the day to recharge the system before being fed in again the following day. In public life, the stated intention to 'spend more time with my family' has become a euphemism for being sacked, but in reality it is not such a bad idea. Over time our priorities change and being able to address the work/life balance has become an important issue – especially for younger managers who may have a working partner and for whom the creation of personal wealth is no longer the principal objective. We sub-titled this book, *A Career of Choice* because that is what Interim Management can offer. You can decide which assignments you want to take, where and when you want to work and how you want to manage your own professional and personal development. It is most definitely not always easy, but at least the choice can be there for you.

Skillset

I started off with a vague, general impression that the skillset of the new breed of Interim Managers has improved. And to test that idea I analysed a sample of the 2000 interviews that I have conducted over the past 10 years and sure enough there were significantly more first degrees, MBAs, and professional qualifications in the second five years than there were in the first, (although some were from institutes and institutions I have never heard of!). One must accept that, in itself, more paper qualifications does not mean that they are necessarily better qualified to met the clients' needs. Yet significantly there is a widespread perception amongst the Service Providers that the skillsets available have improved. One explanation I can find for this is that people now have learned to describe themselves in different ways.

Years ago I interviewed a man who had been the chairman of an overseas subsidiary of a very major financial services company. When I asked what he had done he said,

'I was chairman of xxxxx in Jamaica'

'Yes but what have you achieved?'

' I was chairman of xxxxx in Jamaica for 10 years'.

And that was it. I was expected to know or guess the rest and find him an assignment on the strength of that!

I think today people are much more open and confident about being judged by what they have actually achieved – not what they were, or think they were. Going back to one of our earlier definitions, Interim Managers are well qualified executives with technical or functional skills, usually some general management experience, having operated at or near board level and often significant specialist expertise as well. It is these areas of specific expertise and achievement that people are much more open about discussing and indeed emphasising these days. Being say a finance director is not enough; being a finance director who has also, say, successfully floated two companies on the Alternative Investment Market tells me a lot more about what they have actually done and can do.

So while I think it is unproven to say that the skillset of Interim Managers has improved since the early 1990s, there is now a much greater openness about discussing one's achievements and track record, so that it *seems* to have improved. However, combine that with better motivation for moving into the industry and a stronger commitment to the lifestyle and you can see why Interim Management is set to become an important executive resourcing service for the 21st century.

Summary of Chapter 2: The changing nature of Interim Management

1. Interim Management used to be seen as the last resort of the redundant executive. That has changed.
2. The average age of practicing interims has dropped and many younger people are considering it as a career option.
3. The motivation of interims has improved dramatically and it is seen now as being a 'career of choice'.
4. Whilst it would be unfair to say that the skillset of interims has necessarily improved, people are much more open about discussing their *achievements* as opposed to the positions they have held.
5. The combination of reducing age, improved motivation and demonstrable track records of success by Interim Managers contribute to IM being seen as the strongest-growing executive resourcing service for the 21st century.

3 How big is the market?

Let's assume for the moment that you are cautiously coming round to the point of view that Interim Management could be the next career move for yourself. Maybe you like the lifestyle option, and in theory it could meet your personal and financial objectives. A very proper question to ask though, is:

Is there enough business out there for me to be confident of making a living?

Really of course there are two interrelated questions here:

Is there a large, active demand out there?

And

Can I get a piece of it?

This chapter is primarily concerned with a quantitative and qualitative assessment of the current marketplace. *The book as a whole is the best guide we can offer to help you decide your own potential.*

There are some surveys of the market, some more or less educated guesses, some projections from the published turnover of 'major' players, (actually quite small businesses, really), but so far no one has published an authoritative or commonly agreed value or volume for the market for Interim Management. If you are just starting out, this will no doubt seem slightly alarming. But once you understand why this is, it will seem very understandable – and perhaps less alarming. But do be aware that *WHAT FOLLOWS IS OUR OPINION!*

Tackling the problem

Once you start to get to grips with how one goes about assessing the size of a market such as Interim Management, the reasons for uncertainty become fairly obvious. The difficulties arise from two directions:

1. The ways in which assignments – work – are obtained.
2. Defining the 'Management' element – i.e. price.

Paths to market

There are three ways to get work in this field:

- *Direct* – through your own efforts and contacts. Your contract is between your company and the employer.

- *Indirect* (1) – via an Interim Service Provider, who acts as an agent. Your company's contract is with the ISP, who has a matching contract, at a marked-up price, with the employer. The ISP may or may not be a member of the Interim Management Association.
- *Indirect* (2) – where the 'agent' is not a recognised ISP – perhaps a consultancy, or a recruiter.

The direct/indirect paths

When you first start out you are probably still relatively high profile in your niche, a known player in your field. All your former colleagues and competitors have become potential clients, who could benefit from using your services for a time. It may even be that you have a particular skill set, or an area of knowledge/expertise that they have envied for years, and this is the opportunity they have been waiting for. In our experience, *two thirds or more of the work you get in the first year or two* will come *directly*, from your own contacts. As you work through the potential of your personal connections however, you may well find that you need to cast your net progressively wider. The 'Marketing' aspects of getting work become more onerous, and the advantages of getting someone else to do it for you become more appealing – and by a nice piece of serendipity you become more attractive at that point to the various agents, because of your hard-earned experience – 'been there, done that, got the scars'. At this juncture a higher proportion of work tends to come indirectly.

One ISP has been surveying Interim Managers and clients consistently over a good number of years. His studies indicate that, on average, between *two and three times as many assignments are placed directly* as via agents. Looking at this another way, the Interim Service Providers who belong to the Interim Management Association are estimated to account for only about a quarter of the total reported market. (So they have a good way to travel in the process of selling the idea that the quality control and professionalism and width of choice they offer are worth the perceived premium for their service.)

It might seem that we could straightforwardly get a value for the market from the above insight, by looking up the turnover of the ISP's, and multiplying by a factor of four. However, there are constraints that make using Companies House data quite difficult:

- A number of ISP's are sections of larger, diverse businesses, which do not provide convenient analyses of their turnover.
- Most ISP's report as 'turnover' the sum of payment to Interim manager and mark-up to client, i.e. the total amount invoiced to

client. *But some leave the Interim to invoice the client for work done, and themselves only invoice their own fee.*

- Once one starts to consider that section of the 'Indirect' market which is outside the strict definition of Interim Service Provider – e.g. consultancy organisations, executive recruiters, professional bodies – figures become not much more than guesswork.

Price – what counts as 'management'?

By convention, Interim Service Providers currently use an invoiced daily rate to client of £500 per day as the lower limit of 'Management', for the purposes of defining Interim Management. A glance at our Chapter 8, 'Pricing for Profit', will tell you that this roughly covers jobs at a level where the full-time salaried employee equivalent will be around £50,000 p.a. In London and the South-East of England, the threshold will be higher, and elsewhere often quite a bit lower.

Some genuine research + some heroic arithmetic = an answer

An authoritative publication specialising in talent management put together a list of the 'Top 20 Interim Service Providers'. This survey indicated that the 'top 20' accounted for two-thirds of ISP turnover. The market is very fragmented, with no dominant providers. Summarising the turnover of the IMA group, we get a figure of around £100 million; add a quarter for Interim Service Providers who are not in the IMA, and we get an 'agency-brokered' total of £125 million, and hence a total 'cost-to-employer' market of £500 million.

A calculation of volumes

It is generally accepted that an *average* Interim Management assignment lasts about 100 working days. If we assume that, with a threshold cost of £500 per diem, the *average* daily cost to the employer is likely to be in the region of £600, then the average assignment is likely to be worth (£600 × 100) = £60,000. So there are probably about 8.000 assignments a year, (i.e. £500 million divided by £60,000).

And some advice about fishing

'Drop your hook where the fish are' is the first and most important rule of Marketing. *It is a fact that companies employing more than 1,000 staff are, on average, significantly more likely to understand the value of using an Interim.* So go fish!

Prospects

Traditionally, a company that actually needed an Interim manager would, faut de mieux, have called in a consultancy to do the job. Our belief is that a considerable proportion of the work presently done by 'consultants' could be more cheaply and more effectively be done by Interims. The value of consultancy business runs into the tens of billions, so interims will be chipping away happily at the edges of that sector for many years without making a significant dent. Internationally there has been strong growth in Holland, where managers are often used on a series of short-term contracts, probably as a means of evading restrictive employment-protection laws, and elsewhere in Europe there are signs that the sheer usefulness of the Interim Management concept is gradually overcoming bureaucratic restrictions. There is a lively market in the USA, with indications that younger people are choosing the independent lifestyle, but complicated by the fact that the sheer distances involved make for distinct regionality, and the word 'interim' has itself been high-jacked, to some extent, for lower-level temping.

Demand by function

This is where it gets really tough. It's a fact that Interim Service Providers have on their books, (or rather on their hard discs), people of every function, including the proverbial left-handed banana-bender. The *numbers* of each kind of manager offering to join vary quite significantly over time. A few years ago there were huge meltdowns in Manufacturing, at which time Production and Engineering people were in heavy over-supply. Then there was a fashion to shift Human-Resource Management back from the specialists to the line-managers themselves, so Personnel Directors were plentiful. Then came the flood of EU over-regulation to be absorbed and coped with, and the HR people got masses of Interim assignments. And so on. Read carefully, if you will, the Chapter 6 on MARKETING, and the importance of finding your niche position. *If your niche is strong enough, you will find work.*

Interim Management in the global economy

Sound like a good title for a book! But seriously, it used to be thought, quite logically perhaps, that Interim Management would develop, over time, as a contra-cyclical phenomenon – i.e. that when the economy contracted, and 'regular' employment and recruitment fell, Interim work should increase. Sounds logical. Sadly, experience shows that, when employers hit a rough patch, they just batten down the hatches and throw overboard all 'unnecessary' baggage. Sounds familiar?

Summary of Chapter 3: 'How big is the market?'

1. IN OUR OPINION employers in the UK spend about £500 million a year on this service. A quarter of this goes via agents of various kinds, including the specialist Interim Service Providers. The balance is placed directly with the individual's company.
2. Defining 'manager' as 'jobs worth a fulltime equivalent of £50,000 +', there are about 8,000 Interim Manager assignments a year.
3. Most work comes from companies employing more than 1,000 staff.
4. There are opportunities for every function – the stronger your niche, the better the chances of work.
5. Demand varies generally with trends in the wider economy, but there is plenty of room for growth.

Part Two

Help for the Lonely Interim

$\left(4 \right)$ *Is it for me?*

'Permanent' employment is now a myth

These days it makes little sense to talk of 'permanent employment', meaning a job that will continue for years and years , perhaps leading to a comfortable retirement. Whether you have a salaried job, or you work for organisations on a self-employed fee basis, or you own and run your own company, *your income is only truly secure for a few months ahead*. Companies, even governments, have to face the reality of globalisation, and competition for limited resources. Ageism does exist, and the 45-plus executive on a nice salary is often the natural target for cost-saving economies. Perhaps you are in this bracket, and you are reading this book, 'just in case'. Or perhaps you are getting fed up with corporate life, and wondering what the alternatives are. Might INTERIM MANAGEMENT be the answer? In this chapter and the next we'll be offering a little inexpensive career-counselling.

Don't jump until you know where you will land

If you are absolutely determined to 'go independent', it still makes sense to do all your preparatory work from the security of paid employment. And if you don't really want to go out into that cold world, but think that you might be forced to, it makes even more sense to *get prepared*.

Watch out for the warning signs

The new broom – for the individual executive, the most common warning signal of possible severance is the arrival of a new boss. By definition, you will be under suspicion as a survivor from the ancien regime. You may think you are indispensable. In truth, you actually may be indispensable – *given all the current assumptions about the way the business should be run*. BUT the whole purpose of appointing a new boss will probably be to challenge all those comforting assumptions. And if they go out the window, how long may it be before you follow?

Tough trading – if you're lucky, you might have regular sight of cash-flow information and trading reports. But if you don't, you should still be alarmed if there are frequent emergency Board Meetings, or if suppliers hold back deliveries until the cheque clears. STAY ALERT! These are often the warning signs that tough action will soon be required.

Don't bury your head

If there are storm cones out, polish up your preparations. Get that CV brought up to date, start considering your alternatives. Do you know how much notice you are entitled to? What might your severance pay be? Face the simple reality that it is better to be looking for another way to earn a living while you are being paid by your current employer, rather than while you are sitting at home burning up your precious capital.

That greener grass may be a bottomless bog

It may be that you are not under any particular threat, but just feel fed-up with your current job. You wonder what your prospects might be if you go for something entirely different.

You might strike lucky! On the other hand, it's long odds against. If you work in a large company, the likelihood is that another large company will not be very different. While a small company will be more than suspicious of your 'feather-bedded' history. This applies the other way round, too. If you work for a smallish company, the next one will likely as not be equally demanding. By the same token, large companies will disparage your lack of big-company experience.

The smaller the jump, the softer the landing

By this I mean that the best prospects are the nearest. It pays to refine your CV so that your 'niche' is obvious, (see the Chapter on 'Marketing'). The best chance of finding another job is likely to be in a similar role to your present one, in a similar industry. You might say to your partner, 'I have managed teams in Manufacturing, so I can manage teams in Engineering.' But that won't wash in the tough marketplace that is executive job-search/assignment hunt. Put yourself on the other side of the desk – would you take a risk with such a candidate, when there are lots to chose from *who have done it already?*

Death by the 1000 sheets

A quick word about that market in executive jobs, particularly those newspaper advertisements. They are not usually fraudulent – but it is easy to deceive oneself through over-optimism or ignorance.

A typical advertisement will draw between 200 and 500 applications. That's the *1000 sheets of CV's.* Allowing 30 seconds to scan a sheet, that would require 500 minutes – a very long day's work for an expensive executive recruiter! In practice, that doesn't happen. A junior PA is given a set of filters to apply. For example:

Must be under 40,

Must have experience in our industry/our customers/our suppliers

Must have a degree

Must know our IT system

Etc, etc, etc. With any luck, the recruiter will still be left with a couple of dozen close fits for the post. He will invite perhaps half of those for interview, and extract a short list from that for presentation to the client. Where will that whole process leave you and your application? Take my advice, only apply for jobs that fit your CV like a glove – and if you want employment, read the section in 'Selling' about Networking. It's the way to go!

There's a great deal in the next chapter about the art of constructing a convincing CV, and a lot of good examples in Appendix VI.

Going independent

Money, money, money – know the facts

An essential part of planning your career strategy has to be a detailed examination of your income, your capital assets, and your outgoings. Start by completing a Survival Budget, which should be analysed into 3 categories:

BASIC NEEDS, e.g. Roof and food

IMPORTANT NEEDS, e.g. car, telephone, school fees

DESIRABLES, e.g. holidays, presents, TV, restaurant meals

BID for short.

Most people are staggered to find how little they really need to survive, perhaps for months. Whether you are planning to jump, or expecting to be pushed, a knowledge of your *true financial status and prospects* can be very empowering! Rough it out now:

BASIC NEEDS INCLUDE: **Annual Cost**
Mortgage/rent and rates
Water, power, heat
Telephone, car, maintenance
Insurance/assurance/National Insurance
Housekeeping/food
Sub-total

IMPORTANT NEEDS include:
TV/newspapers, School expenses
Hire purchase
Sub-total

DESIRABLES include:
Clothes
Travel
Holidays
Subscriptions
Entertainment
Sub-total

Notice that I do not invite you to produce a grand total just yet! Instead, now set down the income you can be reasonably CERTAIN of receiving over the next twelve months, e.g.:

Partner's income
Income from savings/investments
Pension(s)
Rent-a-room (Why not?)
Severance
Notice payments
Total Income

If you are living in a house with an exceptional capital value, might it make sense to sell up and live somewhere cheaper, maybe without a mortgage to weigh you down? Are there other ways you can reduce your outgoings?

Obviously you now compare the income total with the prioritised sub-totals of expense, to arrive at a reliable assessment of your chances of financial survival during those vital first months of going independent, when you must assume that you have outgoings, but no extra income from fees. I hope you are looking at:

The 'good news' budget

I can tell you, from long experience, that under the stress of a sudden severance, most people freeze like a rabbit in the headlights, and are quite unable to carry out the process described above. Hence my advice to BE PREPARED – DO IT NOW!

I remember a 53 year old MD of a small division, 25 years with the corporation and a handsome salary package. One morning the Group HR Director arrived in his office, told him he was being made redundant, asked him for his office and car keys and watched him being escorted off the premises. Clumsy, insensitive, barbaric even, but it does happen. Maybe you can imagine how he felt when he got home – branded a failure, no job, no income, perhaps never to work again? I met him the next day, and he was still trembling, alternating between panic and rage.

Fortunately I had been given the details of his severance package, which was not ungenerous. There was an accrued pension, which he could start drawing immediately, or allow to build up further, or take a transfer value into another scheme. I made him sit down at a table with his wife, and we drew up a rough Survival Budget.

After half an hour they were smiling at one another! His pension, if he triggered it now, would provide almost half his current income – more than half when the lower tax-take was factored in. He could relax, and take his time to consider how to plan the rest of his life. They could survive!

Analyse, take advice, take your time

When you are faced with the prospect of suddenly leaving your employment, you might think of yourself as like the powerful engine of a goods train that has been suddenly decoupled from the loaded wagons it has been pulling for so long. The pressure of your daily routine was also a kind of anaesthetic that stopped you thinking too much about your own future. But things have now changed. Your mind is free to race away, and your fears will run riot too. So ANALYSE your financial situation, slowly and carefully. TALK to people you trust, take ADVICE. And above all **do not act precipitately**, especially in matters affecting your lifestyle and your finances. Put all your funds in a safe place, for months usually, until you are absolutely certain that your imagination is safely under control.

Include your family in the plan

From the day you cease employment, your partner's lifestyle will be transformed too. Instead of you being away from the house for 80% of the time, you might well be at home for 80% of the time. Whether it shows or not, your partner will be at least as anxious about the future vas you are. So forget any nonsense about keeping your troubles to yourself. Whether you go for another job, or down the rocky road to independence, there will be disasters and disappointments ahead. And if you have played the strong, silent type, don't be surprised if you're told to get on with it! So encourage your partner to share the uncertainties of the planning with you. Together you can learn to ride out the rough patches and get on with the search for paid work – and it can help a lot if you have a committed taker of messages with a good telephone manner.

Health is critical

When you go independent, your income is closely tied to your ability to work – anytime there is work available – and your income simply stops if you are injured or ill. Moreover you can expect the pressure of having to sell yourself as a service, day after day after day, to generate an exceptionally high level of stress. Especially if your finances are less comfortable than our previous example, and you know that the clock is ticking as you consume precious capital. So get a really thorough check over of every aspect of your health. When you can afford it, think about your limited company providing you with private medical insurance, so that you do not have to wait for treatment if a problem arises. And explore too the interesting field of 'key-man' insurance, which would provide an income when you cannot work. All tax-deductible!

Summary of Chapter 4: Is it for me?

1. 'Permanent employment' is now a myth.
2. Be ALERT to the company's performance – especially when a new boss arrives.
3. Do not jump without *knowing* where you will land.
4. PREPARE – make a lean and mean Survival Budget – it can be very reassuring. Calculate, do not guess. Avoid quick decisions about money.

5. Family support is vital. Share the pain and the gain. Get your partner to read this book too! (He or she might have a vital contribution to make.)
6. Until you're used to it, the independent life is exceptionally stressful – get your health checked – *now!*

5) *You – as a business*

It takes time – lots of time!

And time costs money. Suppose you allow that you will need six months of selling to land your first contract, then say another two to three months before the first contract payment is in your bank account. Go back to the Survival Budget in the previous chapter. How much does it cost you to survive for nine months with no income? That's a guesstimate of the amount of money you are putting at risk by going independent. £15–20,000? A sobering thought, perhaps – though the alternatives are not without risk either.

Shortening the odds

If all your experience has been in large, heavily structured organisations – for example: the Royal Mail, British Telecom, the Civil Service, the National Health, be quite cautious about 'going independent'. *Especially if you think you will need to find customers outside of your corporate experience.* Successful independents have a streak of 'odd man out' about them – if you have been comfortable for years in a corporate environment, make sure you explore thoroughly the alternative to independence – staying where you are or getting another job. That will cost time, and therefore money too of course, but probably less of both – with less chance of total disappointment.

Attributes of the natural independent

Not everyone who succeeds has *all* the following attributes – but the more of them that seem to fit yourself, the more confidence you should have. And vice-versa.

1. A strong desire to own your own business, and a conviction that, with a modicum of research and some luck, you can prove to yourself it is viable *before you jump in*.
2. An identified 'niche' – see the chapter on 'Marketing'.
3. A growing, busy target market.

4. Many influential contacts and a demonstrable competence and reputation in that market.
5. A credible ability to walk into a problem situation and produce a solution, calmly and quickly.
6. Financial independence – an ability to survive for up to a year without further income.
7. Psychological independence – able to live *alone* in a strange city or country, with the only the most casual support of work colleagues.

A SUITABLE CASE

In Appendix II you will find the personal stories of a number of successful independents – indeed the above analysis has been distilled from our acquaintance with many such people. Some certainly did nothing resembling the self-analysis we are recommending, but equally there are many, many others who didn't and who have sunk without trace. So here's a kind of composite of an ideal candidate for independence:

She is 38, a specialist in Computer-Aided-Design, managing a small team and working for a company who provide sophisticated graphics for advertising agencies. After 12 years' experience she is on first-name terms with the key buyers in a dozen agencies, who usually specify her for preference. She could work for a competitor, or directly for a large agency – but she decides there should be an opportunity to set up on her own account.

In confidence, she asks ten of her best contacts if they will employ her as an Interim Manager – less overhead, lower charges. She calculates that if only half say 'yes', she could double her current earnings on 200 days a year.

How you respond to that little scenario could be an interesting test of the likelihood of your succeeding yourself. If you are not happy with the ethics of taking business from one's employer, if you think she is rash to risk her secure employment, then self-employment may not be for you.

On the other hand, if you admire her business-like style and entrepreneurial flair, if you are impressed with her courage, then you are more likely to be suited to the self-employed life yourself. The important lesson to grasp is that, before she jumped, she knew where she was likely to land. It is VERY DIFFICULT to be objective about oneself – even close personal friends or partners can unwittingly mislead you. If you can, try to complete a Psychometric test. (Hint: look it up in 'Google'.)

A TYPICAL INTERIM ASSIGNMENT – THE PEOPLE AND THE CVS

A bank decides that it wants to set up a new call-centre in Scotland, to operate in parallel with the one it has already in Sussex. Because of the pressure of high demand, it cannot spare anyone to lead the project from its current operations, and is persuaded of the benefit of using an Interim. The task will be:

1. Establish a blueprint for the project – site, equipment, staffing, training, operations, costings.
2. Lead the implementation, then help to identify and mentor-in a manager.

It is estimated that there will be 1000 + enquiries per day, some by fax and e-mail, most by telephone and requiring immediate answers – interest rates, charges, balance and credit checks, legal, probate and credit card queries. A daunting job! If you were the client, what would you look for in a candidate?

Experience wins

The answer, above all, is to *look for someone who has done it all before.* You are not recruiting a future employee, who will grow into the job and be a valuable long term asset to the bank. You are 'borrowing a ready made tool'. So you want someone who has *both* banking experience *and* has set up/run a call centre. Sounds a tall order – which is why successful Interim Management Service Providers maintain data-bases of thousands of self-employed independents – so that an exact fit can be found for today's assignment *who is also available to work.* The greater the relevant experience, the steeper and shorter the learning curve will be, with less likelihood of delays and errors.

So ensure your CV shows your experience

Write down what *you* can deliver to some organisation that might need your experience and skill. What kind of organisation would that be? (i.e. what is your **target market?**). Now you are starting to outline the right CV for the marketplace. Think seriously about getting professional help from an Outplacement Agency in psychometrics and CV writing. It is absolutely essential that you identify, as precisely as possible, the 'NICHE' that you intend to occupy as your springboard into independence. Make sure you study the chapter on Marketing, which concentrates on this topic.

Getting the CV WRONG

A senior banking manager had taken early retirement, but discovered after a few months that he was 'missing the action'. He decided he wanted to try to get some work as a Consultant or Interim Manager, and drafted the following front page for his CV:

Richard Cummins, 27 The Poplars, Shreve Bestoming, Gloucestershire, GL22 5BW

   Telephone/Fax: 01273 556 576. E-mail cummins. doc@561229 mobile/pager 0895 347707

   Retired banking executive capable of leading multi-disciplined teams. A team player who believes in democratic staff management and a track record of developing empowered environments. Over 30 years' service in positions where tact and diplomacy have been essential. Experience of strategic analysis of competitive developments in banking services.

   Courses attended include:
   1975–2004 Lloyds Bank internal courses
   1979 Portfolio Fund management
   1984 Ashridge – senior management
   1991 Use of PCs
   Education:
   1958–64 Thornton Primary School, Bristol
   1964–71 Brierton Grammar School, Chichester
   1971–74 Sussex University. B.A.Hons, History
   1980 Finals, Chartered Institute of Banking – Elements of English Law, Book-keeping and Accounts, Company Secretarial Practice, Economics, Banking Law and Practice.

Imagine you are a busy – and expensive – executive or a PA, with dozens of CV.s to read. Does this one grab your attention? Does it promise a benefit that a client might want to buy? Will you wade on through pages 2–6 looking for the good stuff? Sadly, not very likely. However our ex-banker was lucky. He was introduced to an Outplacement professional, who charged him a fee to tweak out a narration of his career and his achievements, and helped him to produce, after a lot of trial and error, the following alternative front page:

And getting the CV RIGHT

Richard Cummins BA Hons FCIB   Tel/Fax 01273 565 723

27 The Poplars, Shreve Bestoming, Gloucs. GL22 5BW

Regional Director of Lloyds Bank, with continuous record of promotions, from cashier to director responsible for 400 retail branches, and 6,000 staff. Strategic competitive initiatives have included leadership of telephone and home banking trials, and development of call-centre based servicing. Business development and promotional experience including new branch openings, staff recruitment and VIP customer liaison.

Key experience/achievements
- Set up first regional call-centre to provide 24/7 customer support for both branch staff and customers direct. Recruited team of 12 specialised customer service telephone staff, plus 30 specialists. We averaged 300 calls per day, with normal guaranteed response within 3 rings and 98% customer satisfaction.
- Obtained sites and opened 35 branches in 10 years.
- etc.

Your CV needs to have that element of focus and punch. Read Chapter 10 about how an Interim Management Service Provider conducts the search and selection process. In this case the 'Industry' will of course be Banking/Financial. The call-centre experience should come out in a 'word search'. You might be concerned that you will need to tailor your CV each time you apply. But if you get your key areas of expertise onto that front page, it should not be necessary to do that. Sometimes a covering letter might be used to draw attention to a special skill. Your CV is the vital document that identifies what you can offer, and who your target customers are. In the chapter on 'Marketing' you will find convincing arguments for FOCUS – choosing a 'niche' *and sticking to it.* As you pick up different assignments your niche will gradually widen – but please accept that you are more likely to win the lottery than you are to get paid work outside of your area of expertise. Just to drive the point home, let's look at the start of another good CV

> **Philip Holland Bsc Chem. MRPS** **01459 606403**
>
> **19 Midway Crescent, Culverton, Sheffield, SH22 4ZY**
>
> Graduate pharmacist with 10 years' experience including biomedical research and development, and drug licensing. 5 years management of busy specialised call centre with 6 staff and sophisticated IT system to manage enquiries from retail pharmacists and GP's.
>
> Skilled analyst able to interpret complex drug-related queries to provide coherent, legally accurate yet jargon-free responses to a national network of doctors and pharmacists, many personally known.

Notice how the CV identifies the potential markets for his services:

1. Pharmaceutical companies.
2. Health Food companies
3. Hospitals and Research Laboratories.
4. Major Retail Chemists.
5. Obviously all his previous company's competitors.

Are there other possibilities?

How about Universities, the Ministry of Health, Specialist Medical magazines. Any one of these might see his CV, together with a proposal to work on a day-rate basis, as an opportunity to get a project off the ground.

Now go to Appendix VI, and read through the front pages of a few more CV's, until you are sure you really do grasp the essence of constructing a good one. A CV that in 30 seconds says

- Who you are.
- What **Benefits** you can deliver. (see Chapter 7 on Selling to understand the vital difference between a Benefit and a Feature.)
- Where you got your experience.
- What factual proof of achievement you can offer.

Doing some research

Now you are armed with a strong CV, it is time to seek some exposure to the marketplace. An easy way to start is to approach half a dozen members of the Interim Management Association with your CV to see if the are willing to register you (see Chapter 10). If you get several negatives, find out why and perhaps reconsider the whole plan! Assuming the answer is 'yes' however, do not expect an interview or any immediate prospect of work. At least though you now know that, if the right assignment comes along, you will be considered. Instead of waiting, you will be pushing on with the next stage – approaching prospects. How you go about that is discussed at length in Chapter 7, 'Selling'. So let's put that task to one side for the moment and get to grips with another vital task.

Make a plan for your business – YOU are the bank!

Start by referring to that Survival Budget, and consider

1. How much you need to bring in to break-even – i.e. avoid depletion of capital – over the year.
2. What level of earnings you would feel comfortable with, assuming you were on fee for 60% of the year, (about 135 days).

Obviously both these numbers will contain an element of guesswork and some 'stretch', but you should have a couple of ballpark figures in mind.

Now set out for yourself a **Business Plan: (some elements are best completed after you have finished a first reading of this book, but are included here for completeness).**

1. The name of your business, and where it will be based.
2. Status, (Sole Trader, Partnership, Limited Company) and owner-ship, (discussed in Appendix VII – Accountant.
3. Summary of what you can offer and who should be customers
4. Pricing structures
5. Potential competition
6. A three year financial projection – sales, costs, cash-flow.
7. A marketing plan.

The above make up the very least you would need to approach a bank for finance. Most likely of course you will be using your own capital – *which is even more reason to go through these essential formalities!* You will also find your Business Plan very helpful when you talk to your bank manager, your accountant, and a friend whose advice you value and respect. Most towns have a Business Link or something similar, a bureau set up by the Government specifically to provide advice to small and start-up companies. Find your local Chamber of Commerce. Use it!

Getting started as a business

Most independents work from home. I trade as 'Dennis Russell Marketing', but if you are not using your own name for your business, you should check with the Registrar of Business Names to ensure there will be no confusion caused by the name you fancy. Tell the Inland Revenue, the DSS, and register with Customs and Excise for VAT. This last is not essential at start-up, but you can recover quite a lot of vatable expense amost immediately, (e.g. the VAT on what you spend on a new PC, office files, stationery, running the car and maintenance,) so why not? The reporting routine is actually quite a useful discipline, and you will have a good two years to reach the VAT minimum turnover. Meantime, would *you* want to use an Interim Manager who didn't earn enough to pay VAT?

Up-front spending – if in doubt, DON'T

A useful rule when starting up is never to spend until you have to. For instance, don't buy an answer phone – they go wrong, and you get better service for nothing from BT 1571. Don't buy a photocopier – use the local copy-shop or a modern printer. DO get a reliable PC with a good printer and an internet connection, you will be producing a lot of letters and e-mail is the preferred method of communication by IM Service Providers. You will need a mobile phone. Have your business cards, letterhead and CV professionally produced on good quality paper. Remember, a decision to use you as a Consultant is probably a £5,000 to £10,000 spend, and an Interim Management assignment is nearer £40–50,000 – so make sure you do not look cheap!

You will probably be driving 30–50,000 miles a year, so you need a reliable, comfortable car – second-hand, say 2 litres. A desk for you and your PC, a chair and a filing cabinet, and that's about the lot. Most expense can be set against tax – which could be helpful if you are intending to recover some of the PAYE already deducted when you were employed!

Bank managers, accountants, solicitors etc.

See Appendix VII for a detailed discussion. *At this stage the important thing to grasp is that the risks of going without, will far exceed the inevitable fees, so DO NOT DO IT YOURSELF!*

Networking

Read about Networking in Chapter 7, 'Selling'. Quite simply it is the basic technique you will use to get work.

Alternatives to networking

It's possible – just – that you could become a very good Interim Manager without doing much in the way of formal networking. Basically, you would need to find other people who will sell on your behalf. A good example would be the members of the Interim Management Association. Sometimes a lucky beginner with a valuable 'niche' skill gets away to a flying start with one or two members of the IMA, and never looks back. You may have colleagues who are already established in their own business and who will welcome you aboard on a 'payment by results' basis. More commonly though you have to build up a track record on your own, and wait to be called.

DO NOT be tempted to pay up front, ever, for an agency service that 'guarantees so many leads a month'. YOU WILL BE DISAPPOINTED.

Read through the chapter on 'Selling', and if NETWORKING is definitely not for you, reconsider the whole project of going independent!

Optimism can be as dangerous as despair

Assuming that you are seriously considering or planning going independent, you need to keep a careful watch on your own emotions. Hope is a powerful driver, and you will tend to hear what you want to hear, ignoring the negative nuances. So be cautious when you are conducting your initial network contacts. WORDS ARE CHEAP. If you had a friend in front of you, asking for your opinion about *his* plan to go independent, you would most probably want to be encouraging, or at least not too discouraging. They call it ' making warm noises'. To sort out the wheat from the chaff, you must expect to go through two or three phases with any business contact before you get near a contract:

Phase 1. 'Can you please give me advice as to whether you think I should have good prospects for my business?'

Phase 2. 'Since we first met, I have talked to a fair sample of people, and it's pretty clear that I can expect to have good prospects. Now I'd like your thoughts on my immediate chances with your company. How would my skills be of value?'

Phase 3. 'I am up and running. That Consultancy project we talked about will take three to four weeks, and cost around £12,000. Can I expect a definite contract within the next 6 months?'

Of course the conversation will be less stark than I have suggested, but I'm sure you grasp the trajectory you should be looking for. You don't expect to make progress of this nature with every contact – just one will do to start with!

Summary of Chapter 5: You – as a business

1. Starting up takes time, effort and money – so plan *assiduously*.
2. Make your mind up about how you will get business.
3. Choose your NICHE rigorously – mostly, work goes to people who can *prove* they have succeeded in that arena previously.
4. Ensure that the front page of your CV tells your story in 30 seconds.
5. Produce a business plan that identifies the potential clients who should value your skills – and expresses that value in a flow of income and costs.
6. Murphy's Law states, 'Any new project takes twice as long as you expected'. Be cautious as well as optimistic.

6 Marketing

Do you need 'marketing'?

I have met Interim Managers who have as much work as they can handle, interesting and challenging work, at daily rates that raised my grizzled eyebrows somewhat. Do they need 'marketing'? Strangely enough, the answer is 'yes', though not 'marketing' in the conventional sense of sales promotion activity. What those successful people all had in common, I discovered was *a fierce focus on delighting their customers*.

So what do we mean by 'marketing'? The answer actually is the same, whether you are a candidate running for the presidency, a giant corporation selling soap powder, or a self-employed independent looking to develop a satisfactory new career. 'Marketing' is, first and foremost, an attitude of mind. I have even heard a well-known guru say "Marketing is an adverb!" He wasn't flaunting his disrespect for the rules of English grammar; he was making the key point that 'Marketing' really delivers success for an organisation when it is an attitude of mind *that permeates everything that is done*. Not simply a way of selling, but a way of deciding what should be offered, at what price, by what routes, to which customers, with what guarantees of performance and so on. All with the single objective of *delighting the customer*.

'Just a moment,' I hear someone say, 'Isn't that the same philosophy as Total Quality Management, or Total Quality Assurance, or whatever the latest buzz-phrase is? YES IT IS! A 'Marketing-oriented' approach means that you do a lot of thinking before you start . . .

Marketing requires that you think

Think first about who your core customers should be – this is *Market-segmentation* and *Niche-selection*.

Think next of exactly who will be placing the order, and what needs or problems that customer may have – this is *Market Research*.

Then think about the 'product' you will be selling – YOU – how can it be moulded, modified, adapted, presented so that the customer sees you as the longed-for solution. You might call this *Product Development*.

When you start an assignment, think how to delight the real buyer
– that's *Product Optimisation.*

*'Marketing' then is the whole process by which you organise your business to
please your customer – and make a profit.* But do not confuse those two
requirements. Still less, do not focus first on the profit. Customers
who feel cheated seldom come back, nor will they recommend you.
The 'game' is satisfying customers – profit is the score.

Marketing for the Interim Manager

How are these grand principles to be turned into a programme of
effective activity for a lonely individual, with himself as the only
possible 'product'? Let's try to see the problem from the point of view
of an imaginary beginner – a debutante into the world of Interim
Management. This is our 'product':

> **48, with a degree in Business Economics from Exeter.
> Trained in Sales with Proctor Gamble, switched into Brand
> Management. Moved to become Marketing Manager at
> Boots Pharmaceutical, then Key Account manager at
> Beecham, promoted to Marketing Director. Head-hunted to
> be Director of Sales and Marketing for Wedgewood, later
> GM of Wedgewood North America. For the last 3 years
> Managing Director of a family-owned Silverware business in
> Sheffield, England, which has now been sold to a French
> competitor, producing a year's pay as severance.**

All wholly imaginary, of course, but not untypical. Here's a pretty
impressive Marketing professional, with solid General Management
experience too. Surely he – or is it she? – is not going to have a
problem finding work? Well, yes, there is a difficulty to be overcome.
You see, like many finance managers, personnel managers, systems
managers, it's 'obvious' to our character that because of that
well-proven professional expertise, one can be effective in almost any
business activity – manufacturing certainly, but also retailing, health
services, tourism – really any field that could benefit from some
marketing nous. Right?

Not so, unfortunately. If you think that way, it probably means that
your mindset is still on employment, rather than operating as an
independent. You are still seeing the market for your sevices as it was

when you were 28. But now you are 38, 48, or 58, and the market wears a very different face for you.

1. TIME – when you went after that new job as a 28 year-old, you saw the opportunity to grow, whilst the employer saw the opportunity to benefit from investing in a resource that would develop and improve over the years, so justifying the cost of your learning period.

INTERIM MANAGERS DO NOT HAVE SUCH LUXURY. The employer is paying for performance, by the day, and *expects instant achievement.* You will be expected to find your way around in hours, and be making significant proposals/decisions in days. YOU CAN'T DO THAT IN AN INDUSTRY YOU DON'T KNOW.

2. COMPETITION, competition, competition! People who are looking for work tend to be somewhat self-centred, (to put it mildly). They look at every job as *something they could do* – if only they were given the chance. Partners and friends often encourage this laudable 'can-do' approach, as an important bulwark against the ever-present menace of the demon despair. BUT IT'S A MISTAKE. Yes, you could probably do it, given the chance. But unless the task is close to your core competence/experience, there is a COMPETITOR out there who is better equipped – because he did something very similar, very successfully, just last month. Be honest now, if you were the employing manager, and you needed to guarantee to the Board that this £75,000 investment, (yes, 100 days @ £750 per day) will produce the required result, which would *you* buy? So, what's the trick?

Marketing for interims is NICHE MARKETING

If you take away from this book only one piece of enlightenment, let it be this:

As your personal marketing strategy, make a firm, unshakeable decision to concentrate on the business area in which you can present yourself, today, as 'one of the best and most experienced.' I say to beginners,

"Imagine that your CV had to begin with the words 'I am the world's expert in . . .' what would follow?"

Go on, don't be modest – this is Marketing!

So what advice do we give then to our imaginary beginner? We say "Think of your *Market Segmentation* as a target, a bullseye surrounded by concentric circles,

At the centre – *all* the silverware makers.

The inner – *all* the makers of fine china.

Next – a little creative imagination might ask the question 'what need/motivation are silver and fine china satisfying?' Then we add *all* the makers of Prestige Gifts to our target".

And so on. Already the number of potential buyers of our beginner's services runs into hundreds – yet he can have confidence (and what an asset that is when you are selling) that he can arrive on an assignment and start to perform within days.

Beginners from other disciplines – operations, finance, personnel, systems, legal – are less tied to specific industries/markets than marketing people. But nevertheless my advice to them (as beginners) would always be the same. Target first the business or industry you know best – its competitors, its suppliers, its customers. Get a good reputation as a sound achiever in your niche, and allow the market itself to widen your field as you progress. Keep selling yourself !

Market Research – for beginners

Having identified our target market conceptually, the next step is obviously to identify some people who might actually become buyers of you, the product. Put it another way, we've got a strategy – how about some tactics?

Start with the known.

It is not necessary or desirable to start with formal research – at least, nothing more formal than going through your old diaries and collections of business cards to jog your memory. Because the reality is that most managers 'know' dozens, perhaps hundreds of people in business. This is your potential NETWORK. And NETWORKING is the key business development activity for the Interim Manager. We go into this in some detail in the next chapter, on Selling.

Product Development – for beginners

In a broad sense, you've done that already! Or at least you should be well aware of how to do it:

1. Your 'market segmentation' activity focussed your attention on identifying that niche you can occupy with most confidence; that combination of industry/function/special experience/skill where you are 'one of the best there is'.
2. Chapter 5 offered some specific advice on how to package your personal niche position in the form of a CV *tailored for Interim Management*. There's much more detail about the vital subject of CV's in Appendix VI.

3. Identify those first half-dozen networking contacts very, very carefully. Ensure that your approach letter and CV are really relevant to their probable needs. Think of yourself as a specialised and fairly expensive piece of capital equipment, and be sure you understand what procedures an Operations Director, say, would go through before placing the order. (If you don't understand this process, FIND OUT).

Engaging an Interim Manager is typically a £50–100,000 spend, and often the expected leverage – or risk – runs into millions. So it is a serious purchase or investment, and your 'product' is likely to be bought on the basis of *what you will achieve for the buyer.*

Product Optimisation – for beginners

DON'T GET LAZY! After that first assignment – and every subsequent one too – modify your CV by including what the requirement was, and what you achieved. Be sure to sign off warmly with the person you will be asking to provide your next reference. Ask if your new CV could be circulated around the group. Ask if there is anyone you could contact. (That's networking again!)

Be honest – were there aspects of the assignment when you knew you were out of your depth a bit? How could you deepen or widen your expertise?

DIY or GSE?

So far we have discussed Marketing as a Do-It-Yourself activity. Does it have to be? After all even the largest corporations use specialist consultancies and advertising agents to identify and reach out to potential customers. Why shouldn't an independent **Get-Somebody-Else?**

You can, of course, indeed we strongly recommend that you do. Read Chapter 10 on dealing with Interim Management Service Providers, (agencies), and also Appendix III about the Interim Management Association. But never neglect your DIY marketing activity – the better you do your marketing homework, the better prepared you will be when a Service Provider comes calling to see if you might fit their next shortlist. An intermediary agency markets itself – not you as an individual. It then *sells* you, *provided you fit really well the niche identified in their brief for the assignment.*

Summary of Chapter 6: Marketing

1. Everyone needs 'marketing'.
2. Marketing is an adverb – an attitude of mind that infuses everything you do – concerned with delighting the customer.
3. For the Interim Manager, 'marketing' is about identifying and exploiting **a tightly-focussed NICHE**.
4. Start with the KNOWN – colleagues, customers, suppliers, and NETWORK (see next chapter).
5. Ensure that your CV communicates, in strong, plain language, the kind of benefit you will deliver.
6. Improve your 'product offering' at every opportunity.
7. Consider carefully the cost/benefit balance of inviting a number of members of the Interim Management Association to include you in their sales activities.

7 Selling – and how to enjoy it!

The worst part of the job?

In my daily routine when I was working for a business that managed a portfolio of Interim Managers in order to provide an IM service to employers, I met a lot of Interim Managers of course. Some were very experienced, some beginners. Some were salesmen – business developers – by profession, but most worked in other functions, such as finance, manufacturing, engineering, IT and general management.

FACT: I never met one who actually enjoyed the 'thrill of the chase', by which I mean the activity of getting and maintaining a flow of assignments for oneself. Most put up with the need to sell, some found it unbearably painful and relied wholly on Service Providers and other third parties, like my own business, to find opportunities for them.

Why is this? Are we, as a nation, naturally averse to self-promotion? Would one expect to find Americans or Australians much more comfortable with it?

Probably not, because when you think a little harder about it, you find that, for a typical independent, getting work can be broken down into *two very different activities*:

1. Getting a hearing
2. Getting the assignment

Neither is easy of course, but anyone who had tried it will confirm that '1' is an order of magnitude more difficult, more irritating and more stressful than '2'. The latter involves having a meeting with people at your own level, using your imagination to understand their possible need, and comparing that with your own skills and experience. That process can be stimulating and entertaining – even if you don't get the work. But getting those all-important first meetings . . . Why is that activity so frustrating and tedious?

It ain't what you do . . .

Cast your mind back to those halcyon days in your comfortable office in that comfortable corporation that once employed you. I expect that you – or your PA – received letters every day, phone call after phone call from people who wanted to sell you something. Assuming you weren't employed as a buyer, specifically tasked to interview potential suppliers, how many got to speak to you, even over the phone? Precious few, I'll bet. Because the vast majority were filtered out, since *they were not selling something you were in the market to buy* – at least not at that time. A well-trained PA might put some letters or brochures in a file for future reference; probably most go straight into the waste bin. How do you evade that trap?

It's the way that you do it . . .

For a start, do not produce a brochure. Your CV will do fine, provided you have carefully followed our guidance on how to prepare it.

Next, DO NOT TALK TO STRANGERS. Not in the early stages, anyway. Begin by writing down the names of six people who know you, preferably on first name terms. Ideally they should come from businesses in or near the core of your market segment. They should be people who carry some weight – Director and Managing Director titles are ideal.

Now write a personal letter to each along the following lines, (but in your own inimitable style):

Dear James,

You may perhaps have heard that I am leaving Sunnilands plc, and I have been giving some thought to what I should do next. One serious possibility is that I might set myself up as an independent consultant or Interim Manager.

This is unknown territory for me of course, and I really would appreciate some advice. If I call Janice next week, do you think she could fit me in to your coffee-time one day? Best regards, Dennis Russell

DO NOT enclose your CV. Take it with you. Take several copies with you! When you meet James:

1. *Ask* as many questions as possible about his business – GOOD LISTENERS MAKE GOOD SALESMEN.
2. DO NOT ask for work, (still less ask for a job.) He will ask you, if you fit a need.
3. Tell him as much as he wants to know about your plans – especially about your chosen NICHE. Seek his comments and advice about your CV.

4. MOST IMPORTANTLY ask him to suggest two or three other people whose advice could be helpful.
5. Take that advice, 'James has suggested, etc.'

Suppose you started with six approaches, and say four were helpful. Now you have eight, possibly twelve people to approach – *with the benefit of a personal referral.* In case the penny has yet to drop, this process is called . . .

NETWORKING

Most of us have been doing it in a casual, unsystematic way all our lives. I am recommending that you make a science of it! With a little expertise – and some luck of course – you will never again be canvassing perfect strangers; never again will you try to sell your product to people who have no interest in buying. On the contrary, you will be talking, as an invited guest, to people who, at the very least, are likely to be intrigued by your plans, and probably flattered to be consulted.

Networking is logical

For Interim Managers, networking is the effective tool for business development for two simple reasons – it is *personal,* and it is *small-scale.*

Personal is important, because the 'product' you are offering is not tangible and is therefore difficult to evaluate. It exists only in the future – in the stream of benefits to your customer that will flow only if he uses you. For most of us, the best way to assess such an intangible is from the recommendation of someone we know and trust – i.e. personal referral.

Small-scale is also very relevant. A salesman with a hungry factory to feed needs order after order after order. He needs therefore to achieve maximum exposure for his product. But that is not your problem at all. You will probably be quite pleased to sell 100 paid days in your first year – say between one and two typical assignments for Interim Management. My expectation would be that *if you can generate between 10 and 20 networked meetings you will get at least one assignment* – and be set up with the contacts and referrals to launch a successful new career.

What happened to that 'chase'?

At the beginning of this chapter I said that few interims, in our experience, enjoyed the 'thrill of the chase'. Perhaps the real reason for this is that getting work is not a bit like a chase or a big-game hunt at all. A much better metaphor would be *farming*. The diligent independent worker identifies a fertile area, turns over the ground, plants seeds in the form of ideas, fertilises and waters those ideas with regular contact, and in due course reaps a harvest *and plants all over again*. Perhaps not as exciting as the chase – but a lot more profitable!

When does the real selling start?

You remember that I made the important distinction between 'getting a hearing' and 'getting the assignment'? Both are vital aspects of selling, but now we need to look at the second. Let's suppose that your networking has been successful, and you are having a chat with the Group Finance Director of a multi-national engineering firm:

'We could just possibly have something for you to get your teeth into,' he says. 'Bill Wilson is MD of our Specialist Valves division in Southampton. His FD gave notice last week, and we'd be quite happy if he went quickly, as he's to join a competitor. No immediate successors around, so we're going to have to recruit. Meantime there's a lot on. Bill has put up one or two ideas for a stand-in, and I've been scratching around too, but without much success so far. Would that interest you? At a guess, three to six months? Bill's decision of course.'

Three days later you are in the reception area of Specialist Valves Division. How will it go for you?

Selling – the basic skills

1. *Time spent on reconnaissance is never wasted* . . . Make sure you know as much as possible about the Group and its divisions. The Group FD should certainly offer you a copy of the latest Shareholders' Report – what does it say about Valves Division? Not very much? ASK before you leave his office. You're no longer asking him for a favour – he's asked you! So naturally it's a sign of your professionalism to ask him in return for information that will make your meeting with the divisional MD more productive for both sides. But don't be tempted

to be too clever. A call to the departing FD might be informative; but it might get back, and lead to a snap 'too-clever-by-half' assessment. But you might expect to be armed with:

What systems/hardware is used?
What is the reporting cycle?
Next Budget due?
Review of current Budget?
Significant Capital/Marketing spends coming up?
Acquisitions? Rationalisations? Disposal even?

2. *Two ears, one mouth* ... Which means that you listen more than you speak. Whether or not you've got the answers to your questions before the meeting, ASK, LISTEN, MAKE NOTES.

3. *Think about possible political scenarios* ... Use whatever information you've gleaned in advance to form an hypothesis. For example:

(a) The divisional MD may have a friend he'd like to bring in. Would that have credibility at Group level?

(b) He may equally fear a Group implant, (=spy). Can you convince him of your professional impartiality?

(c) Is the Group FD's recommendation whole-hearted? Is it beneficial? Might there be a risk of 'not-invented-here'?

DO NOT MAKE ASSUMPTIONS. Try to be sensitive to what may really be going on. You do not of course, want to get involved in any politicking – on the other hand you do not want to get under the wheels of some corporate juggernaut.

4. *Sell* **Benefits** rather than **Features** ... People who have not been professionally trained as salesmen have great difficulty in distinguishing between Features and Benefits. Think, for instance, about a car.

'It has a 2.5 litre engine' is a FEATURE.

'This means that it will pull my caravan easily up Devon hills' is a BENEFIT.

Or think about yourself:

'I have worked in an engineering business' is a FEATURE, (and quite an important one for this assignment).

But 'This means I am likely to know where the bodies are buried' is a BENEFIT, (at least to an honest divisional MD it will be.)

AS PREPARATION FOR THAT MEETING go through your own CV, identifying the FEATURES of your skills and experience that seem relevant. NOW WRITE DOWN the corresponding 'this means that ...' sentence to communicate the BENEFIT to the customer. And I don't mean customers in general, I mean the particular person you will be meeting.

If all this sounds rather artificial and calculating – it's meant to. When you have done it 10 or 20 times it will become second nature – but PREPARATION and ANTICIPATION are the keys to feeling comfortable rather than embarrassed in that selling situation.

'BEEN HERE, DONE THAT, GOT THE SCARS' are the most reassuring things a buyer wants to hear from you. Read carefully Chapter 10, all about how an IM Service Provider goes about its selling process.

To repeat, **previous experience** is the fundamental tool for bridging the credibility gap. And, of course, in the previous chapter about Marketing, that was the principle reason for recommending to you so strongly that you start out from a tightly-defined core **NICHE**.

On occasion you will meet a potential client without your having much idea of what particular issue or problem is going to come up. So the vital preparatory step is that you KNOW YOURSELF. Not many people do, you know, at least not well enough to respond confidently in a live business meeting situation. By KNOW YOUR-SELF I'm not talking about psychological introspection – you've done that pretty thoroughly before deciding to go independent, I hope. I mean KNOW YOURSELF AS A PRODUCT. Know, in detail, all the things you have experienced and achieved over the years, and so you will be PREPARED to relate a selection to the client's problem.

Do not attend interviews

Interviews are for people looking to be employed. You, however, are different now. You are looking for work, at a daily rate, as an independent. So you don't go for an interview, you go to a BUSINESS MEETING. (Which implies that you do *not* expect to be paid expenses.) At this the client explains his need, and you review your 'product range', to see if there is a fit. If there isn't, be honest enough to say so. You might then suggest that you know an IM Service Provider who could help, thus producing a 'win–win' situation whereby the client likes you because you can solve his problem, and the agency likes you because you produce business for them. Magic!

Be prepared for the worst

Not even the sales superstars make a sale every time. *Probably three out of every four enquiries* will just evaporate, either because the client's problem goes away or another solution is found. Sometimes one loses out to a competitive solution. That hurts, always. 'If you can't stand the heat, stay out of the kitchen' is absolutely true for selling. It is especially painful when the 'product' that is rejected is yourself. BUT IT'S NOT PERSONAL. It's business, and the competitor's solution seemed better than yours *on the day*. Sometimes the chemistry is wrong; other combinations of skill and experience seemed a better fit; the client may just go without, as a low-cost solution. If you don't get the assignment, enquire (very, very politely) how the problem will be resolved. Ask yourself, 'Could I have done better?' If so, tuck away that lesson for next time. THERE IS ALWAYS A NEXT TIME.

Is there an alternative?

Not really. Third parties can be helpful in getting you a meeting with an employer to discuss a possible need. But read the chapter about how IM Service Providers work, carefully. You will almost always be one of say three on a short-list. *It's still down to you to make the sale.*

This means that the buyer has to be convinced, by you, that the BENEFITS will outweigh the COSTS.

Summary of Chapter 8: Selling – and how to enjoy it!

1. Distinguish between 'getting a hearing' and 'getting the assignment'.
2. Don't talk to strangers – NETWORK.
3. Networking is effective, because it is personal and small-scale.
4. Good salesmen are farmers, not hunters.
5. Reconnoitre. Get all the possible facts. Be sensitive.
6. Listen. Ask questions. Listen again. And again.
7. Know your 'product'. Know its FEATURES. Now rewrite them as BENEFITS.
8. Previous relevant experience is the most persuasive sales motivator.
9. You now attend Business Meetings, not interviews. *No one makes a sale every time.*
10. **T**here **I**s **N**o **A**lternative!

8   *Pricing for profit*

What shall I charge?

Alternatively, 'What will this customer pay for this assignment?'

Flexibility is everything. Many successful interims vary their daily rates up and down by 50% over the course of the year. But being flexible is not the same as making it up as you go along. There *are* some rules – or perhaps 'guiding principles' would be a better description,

Guiding principles

1. A price for convenience and flexibility

Compared to the rigidities of an open-ended employment contract, with its built-in overheads, bonus, termination cost and so on, clients should – and do – pay a premium for you being available, *flexible*, and able to get the job done *now*. Think, for example, of the cost-per-mile of running a car of your own – say £0.40 for a mile – and compare that with a taxi – say £4.00. A ten times factor! Yet perfectly sensible people own cars, rent cars, and take taxis. Why is this? Because they know that there is a competitive market for these services that keeps a measure of control on the price – and because, at the time, **the value of the convenience outweighs the cost**.

2. The true cost of employment

How much of a premium is reasonable? Start by considering your own needs, which will of course be broadly similar to those of your likely competitors, so that together you make a marketplace for your product.

Let's suppose that, when you were employed, your salary was £60,000 a year. *But that wasn't by any means the true cost of employing you.* There were a host of other costs carried by your employer, which the self-employed has to think about very seriously. For example:

	Annual add-on cost
Employers' National Insurance at 12.2% × £60,000	£7,320
Employer's Pension contribution at 8%	£4,800
Car – lease and running cost	£8,000
Private Health Insurance	£2,000
Bonus	£5,000
Recruitment, (25% spread over, say, 5 years = 5% of salary)	£3,000
Outplacement (15% over, say, 5 years = 3% of salary)	£1,800
Total	£31,920

Not all the above were necessarily incurred when you were an employee. But there could have been lots more – Training, Entertaining, Severance, for instance, and you should certainly estimate the true annual cost of employing you as an executive to be *at least* 'Salary-plus-one-third'. So that would have been £80,000. Work out for yourself which, if any, of those on-costs have gone away because you are self-employed! Divide your total by the 'working days in an average executive year' – (225, allowing for statutory holidays, paid vacations, and a couple of days sick-leave), – and the crude daily rate comes out, in my example, at (£80,000/225) = £356 per day.

3. The price of being available

But there is a further important personal calculation. Research shows that, on average, a diligent, reasonably successful Interim can expect to be in paid work for about 60% of the year. From the buyer's point of view, it is *essential* that these extensive gaps in the work-year come along, otherwise the Interim would hardly ever be available to be hired!

The remainder of the time he is (like a typical actor) 'resting' – i.e. looking for work – or 'rehearsing' – i.e. on a course to keep his skills up to date. So to end up with gross earnings of £80,000 per year, the required daily rate has to include a 'premium for being available', which brings the figure up to (£356/0.6), i.e. about £600 per day. This is your 'standard daily rate'. **Note that £600 is 1% of £60,000.**

The 1% factor

So this little ramble through the costs of self-employment leads us to a very useful rule of thumb, of value for interims and for potential users of interims.

For an average executive salary level, a good Interim Manager will cost, per day, about 1% of the salary rate for the job if it were permanent employment. Research over a wide range of real-life interim assignments shows that this theoretical calculation *in fact holds true in practice.* Actual fees paid worked out at 1.1% of notional salaries.

Does this hold true for a £40,000 job? And for a £120,000 job? Probably not. A more detailed look at the research I mentioned showed that there were some 'lumps' at each end of the scale:

1. At the lower end of the scale the percentage was generally higher – up to 1.3%
2 At the higher end the percentage dropped away from the average, to around 0.75%. An exception would be the high-risk 'corporate rescue' task, where the rate can be open-ended.

What about flexibility?

'OK', I hear you saying, 'I see myself as a £60,000 executive in salary terms, so my standard daily rate is going to be £600 as an Interim. How do I decide when to go for more than that – and when to go for less?'

1. Consultancy pays more

Here's some accumulated wisdom from the history of Interim Management:

'Consultancy is altogether different from Interim Management'

We are not talking here about the multi-layered Consultancy that corporations might buy from a huge Consultancy group, often with historic connections to the top 6 international accountants. Their costs to control and supervise easily add 50–100% to the calculation. But the ordinary consultancy job that you might do yourself directly for a client is still very different from an Interim Management assignment:

1. Getting the job itself involves a substantial (usually unpaid) investment in analysis, in proposal writing, and in sales presentations. This is additional to the standard marketing costs to find the opportunity.
2. The typical consultancy assignment is measured in days, or a couple of weeks – whereas the typical Interim assignment is measured in months. So there is a *much* higher marketing-cost-per-assignment-day for consultancy – which must be factored in to the cost.

3. Consultancy involves not only your man-hours, but also a significant transfer of your intellectual skills – a kind of Capital transfer. You leave behind with your client a valuable piece of your capital, a 'brain-power investment'. Clients should expect to pay for that.

As a rough guide, a typical (say 10-day) consultancy warrants at least a 50% increase on your standard rate. Some assignments fall naturally into a two-stage process, an investigative consultancy exercise at a fixed fee, to be followed by a longer Interim Management assignment at a daily rate to implement your proposals.

2. Beginners get less

You are not going to be surprised to hear that there is a fairly well-established pecking order amongst Interim Managers. Those with two years' experience or more can prove, from a string of successful assignments and enthusiastic references from satisfied clients, that they can deliver. By contrast a beginner can only point to a successful record *as an employee*. So you'll need a substantial customer benefit to offer, in order to make that vital breakthrough into the first assignment.

Don't be proud – CUT THE PRICE! Assuming you started from our £600 per day figure, a price in the £350–400 range should be appropriate. After all even £400 per day is £2,000 per week, paid gross, so that should cheer up the bank manager! Consider setting a progressive target for yourself, say £350 per day for the first assignment, rising to £500 for the third and so on. Be flexible, look for the negotiating potential, once you believe the client is ready to buy. 'If I charge only £350 per day, could you help me by paying my weekly invoice in seven days?'

3. IM Service Providers cannot buck the market

The pros and cons of working through a third party, such as an IM Service Provider, are covered in Chapter 10. Sufficient at this stage to point out that in general an agency will not be able to get a significantly higher price for you than you could have commanded for yourself, had you been able to get that interview. It follows therefore that the Service Provider can only make its margin *if you reduce your standard price according to the rate suggested*. If this worries you, you should not bother to register in the first place. On the other hand, most interims have recognised that such third parties have a useful function in the marketplace, but do read Chapter 10 carefully and make up your own mind. Using their service could help you make that breakthrough, or more likely, improve on that 60% average utilisation factor. If you don't like the terms you don't have to go for interview. But do not play games – **if you agree terms for an assignment with a Service Provider, (which you will normally have to do before you go for interview), you** *must* be prepared to accept the job on those terms if the client chooses you.

Summary of Chapter 9: Pricing for profit

1. You are a valuable potential asset to a client, because you are available, flexible and (above all) effective.
2. Your standard daily rate should be around 1% of your *salaried value* as an employee (but beware: were you underpaid or overpaid?).
3. Consultancy work requires a significant premium per day compared with Interim Management. Don't get confused between the two!
4. Beginners must have a progressive pricing strategy, to offset lack of experience.
5. Third party Service Providers need to make a margin, which you have to allow as a discount from your ideal daily rate if you want their support.

9 Negotiating

Negotiating is a skilled activity, almost indeed an art-form. As any parent will admit, children learn aspects of negotiation at a very early age! Like them, we do it unconsciously every day as we try to resolve problems at work, with family and with friends. At the heart of every negotiation is the recognition of a conflict, actual or potential. We want to achieve position 'x' – someone else wants 'y'. In our imagination, we draw a line between 'x' and 'y', and start to look for a point somewhere between the two which will seem fair to both sides.

I have a quotation pinned over my desk which reads:

Single-handedly I have fought my way into this hopeless mess.

It has a companion:

When you're up to your neck in crocodiles, remember the objective was to drain the swamp.

These are just little reminders that, while *some* negotiating is essential and inevitable, the less obvious you are about how you go about it, the more likely you are to end up with a *strategically satisfactory result*.

What does 'strategic satisfaction' mean? It's a way of reminding you that you can win a battle, but lose the war! Remember always that you are negotiating with someone you may expect to work with for months, sometimes years to come. Once again the appropriate metaphor will be *ploughing and harvesting*, rather than hunting and making a kill. So a satisfactory negotiation ends with both sides feeling a good deal has been achieved, and both sides respecting one another's professionalism. We call that '*win–win*'.

Plan, plan, and plan again

As the saying goes, 'to fail to prepare is to prepare to fail'. It is vital to have thought though, in advance of any meeting, what your personal situation is, and what the implications of that should be for your negotiation. Sometimes you may have found yourself in a fertile furrow, when cash has flowed nicely for a good while. When the question about price is asked, you might then be able to reply. 'I'm just coming to the end of eight months, including a renewal, when I was paid £700 per day', and you just wait for a comment. Sometimes however you've had a lean patch, and you say, 'I know it's important for me to get back on the tools – what do you think would be reasonable?'

Do not be intimidated

When you are dealing direct with a potential client, there seems to be a huge gap in power between yourself, trying to get work that will pay the bills, and this great multi-national with millions in turnover and thousands of employees. Just say to yourself, 'He's got a problem that needs solving, otherwise we wouldn't be having this discussion.' Here are a few tips on how to get a fair deal:

1. DO NOT QUOTE A PRICE, if at all possible, until it's reasonably apparent that there is a deal on the table to go for. That way you have some strength to counterbalance the usually overwhelming power of the buyer

2. IN THE FIRST INSTANCE, QUOTE A PRICE RANGE. Something along the lines, 'Over the past couple of years my daily rate has varied, according to a number of factors, between £600 and £800. Of course short assignments usually qualify for a higher daily rate, and vice-versa. Is that in line with your budget?' NOW SHUT UP! Watch his body language carefully. Does he relax? (= probably you're going to be OK to ask for £700 a day), or does he visibly stiffen? (= he was expecting you to quote £1,500 per week). Possibly it's too difficult to tell. WAIT IN SILENCE FOR A RESPONSE. He may need time to work out a gross budget, say 100 days at £700 per day = £70,000. Unless you are dealing with a professional buyer, the chances are that he is actually less prepared for a negotiation than you are! And always bear in mind that your potential client is very rarely spending his own money. Mostly, the need is to be able to *justify* the price paid. So WAIT FOR AN OFFER OR AT LEAST A COMMENT.

3. An offer means that *the job is yours when you say 'yes'* – it's not going to go away if you now start talking again! Let's suppose that the offer is really too low. What do you do? Remember, his principal need is to justify his DECISION – so help him by explaining the arithmetic that lies behind your business. Sketch out for him, on a piece of paper on his desk, the workings, as set out in the chapter on 'Pricing', and show how you, very reasonably, arrive at that memorable 1% figure. Remind him of the benefits of being able to use you without overheads,

without any other commitment than to pay the daily rate. THEN WAIT AGAIN FOR A RESPONSE. *The worst mistake in any negotiation is to keep chattering. Be patient.*

4. UNDERSTAND THE DIFFERENCE BETWEEN NEGOTI-ATING AND HAGGLING. Mostly, a client is happy if he can show a gain compared with the maximum potential cost, and you are happy if you get 100 days instead of 80, with all expenses agreed. If the deal seems 'good enough', TAKE IT, don't try to optimise. You want the client to feel comfortable about recommending you for another assignment!

Don't forget to include

EXPENSES – not actually negotiable! Your position is that you will need only the same level of expense provision that any comparable manager in the company would get. If divisional directors stay in 3-star hotels, that would be your standard too, (though many interims, who commonly find themselves staying away from home 4 nights every week, find that a homely 'farmhouse-style' B&B is nicer as well as less expensive.) Remember that the self-employed can claim mileage to work as a tax-deduction, but it does no harm to ask the client to pay.

NOTICE PERIOD – important for security for both sides. Get it right! Suppose the client, or you, estimate that the job will take '3–4 months'. Remembering that there are about 20 working days in a month, you might suggest that the contract should read: '60 days, and thereafter subject to 20 working days' notice on either side.' Explain to the client that, if he wants to finish your stint after the 3 months, (60 days), he should simply give notice on Day 40. You could even suggest he puts that in his diary. After that, both sides continue with 20 days always in hand until due notice is given. Be relaxed about this issue, the reality is that nearly everything takes longer than the number you first thought of!

PAYMENT TERMS. Companies like to pay invoices 'end of month following', (at best). You need to do better, because your invoices represent your cash-flow. Try for, ' if I submit my invoice weekly, do you think you could ask Accounts to pay them fortnightly?'

Negotiating with IM Service Providers

This is a specialised kind of negotiation, so you'll find it included in the next chapter, which is all about these intermediaries. You have to be aware that they are business people, who have to protect *their* profitability. But they do want you to succeed!

Summary of Chapter 9: Negotiating

1. Negotiating is the art of finding an acceptable point between two extremes.
2. Look for the 'strategically satisfactory' result, i.e. 'win–win'. You are a good solution to a problem that has to be solved, so do not be intimidated.
3. Hold off talking price until there is a deal to go for. Then quote a RANGE. After that LISTEN, and wait for an OFFER.
4. Avoid seeming to haggle – be reasonable and practical.
5. Details like Expenses and Notice Period should be just that – matters of routine, important, but not to be argued about.

10 Inside an IM Service Provider

What does it do?

Interim Management Service Providers are, at the core, MARKET-ING businesses. Their portfolios of Interim Managers make up the 'product' that they sell. Their customers are, of course, client organisations of every kind – heavy engineers, FMCG manufacturers, retailers, banks, national and local government, the National Health, and so on.

Most managers will have had personal experience of recruitment agencies; many will have met one or more 'head-hunters' – slightly mysterious people who somehow identify a potential candidate for a position, persuade him or her to consider a move, then present the candidate to the employer as the solution to his problem.

AN IM SERVICE PROVIDER DOES NOT WORK LIKE THAT.

Yes, you are the 'product' that the client eventually pays for. But the Service Providers do not go about their marketplace selling you as an individual. Rather they are engaged, competitively of course, in no less than three tough marketing tasks of their own:

1. Informing, educating and persuading their clients of the availability and usefulness of Interims – i.e. developing *total usage*.
2. Persuading clients of the advantages of using a professional Service Provider as the source for Interims – i.e. developing the Service Providers' *share of the total market*.
3. Persuading this particular client that this particular Service Provider is a totally professional, totally adequate, totally cost-effective provider of solutions to today's problem – i.e. developing business for *this particular Service Provider*.

Some IM Service Providers are subsidiaries or offshoots of major businesses, but certainly none could be classified as a large business in its own right. To give you an indication of scale, only the largest would earn as much as £3 million gross margin. So with those three marketing tasks to chew on, it's hardly surprising that they do not generally get around to marketing you personally.

So, how does it work?

There are differences from business to business, but in this chapter we look at the most common methodology:

1. Joining the clubs

Ten years ago the number of potential candidates wanting to register for work as an interim was so great that entry was restricted to those who had already worked successfully as an Interim for a year or two, at least. Then the cycle turned, the number of Service Providers increased rapidly, and candidates were actively recruited – though preference was still given to those with experience. Currently the market generally is tighter once more. Normally you will not be interviewed at entry, (more about that interview later), so the entry process can seem rather daunting and impersonal. But there are some quite specific criteria:

(i) Status

IM Service Providers operate mainly in the field of middle to senior management – heads of function to director and managing director levels, say £50,000 to £150,000 'employed salary' equivalents. There is a preference to 'parachute down', i.e. to use an Interim Manager *at a level below* the highest level reached in employment. So it helps if you have held a job for a few years within those brackets.

(ii) Large organisation experience

It is a fact of life that most IM assignments come from largish (1000 + employees) companies. So that's where most selling effort goes. Potential candidates should have had appropriate experience in such corporations, since someone with *only* smaller company experience is unlikely to be acceptable to those important clients. That's not to say that such candidates cannot succeed in Interim Management – it's just that much more difficult!

(iii) Variety

Provided criteria (i) and (ii) are met, the more variety in a CV the better. Interims need to get assimilated very quickly into new corporate cultures – so proof of exposure to, and success in a variety of differing organisations is a real plus. Proof of lengthy (1 year plus) working in a foreign country can be particularly advantageous – provided you really worked there, and were not just a visiting fireman. The requirement is to have become 'competent in the culture'.

(iv) Commitment – the 'sine qua non'

The Service Provider will need to be persuaded at some point that you intend to remain working as an Interim as *a positive career choice*. Yes, you might be lured astray by an irresistibly attractive offer of employment. But you are most definitely *not* looking for it. *You have crossed over* – instead of looking for employment, and being prepared to accept temporary work as a 'fill-in', you are now a professional independent, looking only for professional assignments as an Interim.

Which club(s) should I join?

In Appendix III you will find a good deal of information about The Interim Management Association. There are some Service Providers of quality who, for technical reasons, are not members of the IMA. There are also some less salubrious businesses who will not be allowed to join. Assuming you are just starting out as an Interim, the best advice is only to register with members of the IMA. That will give you plenty of choice, and a hefty bunch of registration forms, or more likely on-line data-entries to complete.

What happens after I've joined?

In all probability, not a lot. At the outset the Service Provider will:

1. Check that your data-entry is valid and complete. If your qualifications etc are interesting but your CV needs work, you *might* get a call with a suggestion or two!
2. Take up references. A conversation with a senior executive will be 'full, frank and fearless'. Essentially they are finding out what your referee will say when a possible buyer decides not to take their word about you! Choose referees whose words will carry weight. 'Director' titles are preferred.
3. Keep your data secure and accessible on the files, where you will now sit in electronic limbo, waiting to be born anew as a candidate on a short-list.

How can I get selected for a short-list?

Service Providers are pragmatic. They will reach out for you with enthusiasm and alacrity WHEN THERE IS A CLIENT ENQUIRY FOR WHICH YOU MIGHT BE A GOOD CANDIDATE. The search for appropriate candidates against an assignment brief is not for the most part a actually a *selection* activity; it is essentially a process of *'sifting to reject'*, which goes through a series of discrete stages:

1. Parameter search
Usually done quite simply, sometimes by junior staff. They enter the 'must have' requirements for the task. For example, INDUSTRY – e.g. 'must have worked in Manufacturing'; FUNCTION – e.g. 'must have been a Works Engineer'. LOCATION – e.g. 'must live within commuting range of Glasgow'. LANGUAGE – e.g. ' must be competent in German'. There may be several thousand people in the data-base, so such a basic search will possibly throw up several dozen candidates. At the next stage,

2. 'Word' search
Probably another key attribute is entered, such as 'knowledge of PRINCE', (a common tool for managing complex projects). Or it could be 'FRESH FOODS' The object is to reduce the numbers, and tighten the fit.

3. CV browsing
This last filter probably brings the list down to a manageable 5–10 CVs, which are read in detail, and a first short-list is prepared. The executive running the assignment knows that the closer the search comes to finding candidates who can say 'been right there, done exactly that', the more likely the client is to buy. Leaps of 'creative' recruitment are *very* rare in Interim Management. Next step is:

4. Telephone contact
Will seem quite casual, but is actually vital. Is your voice-mail live? Sure? What about the automatic transfer to your mobile – does it work? First question, 'What are you doing currently? Will you be available on such and such a time-scale?' Assuming the answer is 'yes', the assignment will be outlined, and if you are still in the frame there could well be some probing of one or two CV specifics, and a discussion, possibly even some agreement, about ideas on pricing.

5. Interview
Assuming you are not already known, there will be an invitation to meet the Service Provider for interview. This is a business meeting, so Service Providers do not pay expenses! Often the interview becomes a useful coaching activity for both sides – the candidate develops a

personal relationship with the executive, and learns what the client's needs and attitudes might be, and the interviewer learns a lot about the candidate's style and methods.

6. Finally a shortlist

Probably three or four candidates are recommended to the client for a meeting. At that stage the Service Provider will usually adopt an even-handed approach – the client is given a decision to make:

'All these short-listed candidates fit the brief and could do the job. These are their daily rates. Which one has the best chemistry-fit with the user-chooser?'

Can I improve my chances?

The process of arriving at a short-list is not always the same, but what you might call the trajectory of selection, (which you realise is mainly a process of *rejection*, at least until the final stage), will be similar. So, to improve your chances:

1. Don't be lazy about completing the data-entry. The Service Provider has to have a standard format to enable consistent data-capture and adequate recall/access. If you were an IT Director in a building company, that 'Industry' is 'Construction', not 'IT'. If you've had genuine functional experience in Personnel, Production, Purchasing and Methods/O&M at *manager* level, do put in all 4 Functions. 'International Experience' means 'worked there and got the scars to prove it'. If it was in France, say so. Occasional days or weeks in Spain, Germany or the USA belong in the CV proper – not in the parameters.

2. Before you start, review your CV carefully. Does it communicate *what you achieved in each post?* Have you mentioned *by name* for instance each IT Finance system or MRP system you are comfortable with? (Bear in mind how that 'word search' process was used). Don't worry too much about the length of your CV. Unlike recruiters, a Service Provider only has to read those few 'filtered-in' CV's that are likely to match the brief. For your employed career, two or three pages of 'achievements in post' will be fine, plus a similar amount devoted to achievements as an IM, with most weight allocated to the most recent.

3. Update your CV every 6 months, or at the end of each assignment, usually by e-mail – and if you're working in Bangkok, send them a postcard!

Negotiating terms

Most Service Providers do this for you with the client before you meet. Generally the business structure is simple: your limited company invoices the IM Service Provider monthly, (sometimes weekly), and they add their margin and invoice the client in turn.

Expenses are usually claimed by invoice by you directly from the client, although sometimes daily rates will be agreed 'to include travel to work and accommodation.'

Standard practice is to tell the client what each candidate will cost when the short-list CV's are submitted. It follows that you have to negotiate your daily rate with the Service Provider *before the client meeting*. There is an important rule – '*If you go for the meeting, it is on the understanding that terms have been agreed and that if you are selected you will take the assignment on those terms.*'

Fixing your fee – the good news

It's always a good idea when negotiating to have an understanding of the other side's point of view – which is no doubt why you're reading this chapter.

It is assumed that you have read the previous Chapter 8 about 'Pricing'. Did you find it helpful? Logical? Persuasive? Be honest now, if you have recently come out of career employment, didn't that '1%' calculation raise your eyebrows a bit? Somewhat on the high side perhaps? STOP RIGHT THERE! Go over the logic with me once more:

(a) It is very much in the customer's interest that there should be available a pool of active and professional interims.
(b) Interims can only be *active* and *professional* if they work.
(c) Interims can only be *available* if, part of the time, they are *not* working.
(d) Able people will only tolerate the structural uncertainty of irregular work if they are adequately paid.
(e) My '1%' figure is solidly supported both by analysis and by actual practice.
(f) It is accepted that beginners might indeed need to develop a progressive pricing strategy.

So, when the account executive of the IM Service Provider asks what your current rate is, tell him the truth! Perhaps,

'Up till last month I was on contract through A, (one of his competitors) at £550 per day to me.' Or

'You know this will be my first assignment; my last salary was £72,000 a year. What do you suggest is right for this?'

Either way, put the onus on your contact to suggest a daily rate for you. He knows that, working in the client's business, you are likely to find out what rate is being charged for you, which tends to stop the gross margin becoming too fat!

The bad news

The '1%' figure is a very rough and ready calculation. You might interpret it as, 'the fair daily rate for an average Interim Management assignment will be around 1% of the open market salary for the job, if an employed manager were seconded into it'. Given that an IM Service Provider will often aim to 'parachute down' – i.e. put forward candidates who have worked at a level senior to the actual assignment level – the notional salary level might actually be *rather less than your last employment.*

Most importantly, that 'fair daily rate' that you might aim to get if you found the assignment for yourself is also (more or less) what the Service Provider will expect to get for you. Which means that, on average, your daily rate from this assignment will be that much lower, to allow the Service Provider to earn its GROSS MARGIN.

Definition: *GROSS MARGIN is the difference between the cost to the client (the Service Provider's selling price) and your daily rate, expressed as a percentage of that client cost. For example:*

Client pays Service Provider £650 per day for you.
Your limited company charges £500 per day.
Service Provider's GROSS MARGIN is £150/650 = 23%

So why use a Service Provider?

Generalising from the above, your daily rate working through a Service Provider is likely to be lower than you would earn if you were working directly for a similar client. So is the discount worthwhile? Some considerations to evaluate:

WORK IS MORE PROFITABLE THAN INACTIVITY, of course. If you do not have an immediate prospect of work at full rate, it must make sense to consider work at a discounted rate.

QUALITY ASSIGNMENTS ARE HARD TO GET. By 'quality' in this context I mean interesting, challenging work for a prestigious client. The kind of work that will actually enhance your CV, (and so enhance your future prospects). An assignment that lasts months rather than days. Where you don't have to chase payment . . .

SERVICE PROVIDERS LIKE TO RECYCLE. It's a fact of life that they very often include in their short-lists one or two 'old faithfuls' – people who have worked through the company previously, who came back with glowing references which in turn brighten their reputation with the client. So that first assignment might very well lead to a lucrative flow of other business – which is what I meant by 'joining the club'.

ACCESS TO BIG CORPORATIONS IS VERY COMPLEX. One is often told that the average interim finds it relatively easy to get a hearing in smallish, local businesses, say up to £50 million. But only the really effective networkers penetrate the big companies, (who are actually the likeliest to buy). And even then the complexities of multi-level, multi-divisional decision making can be insuperable. Agencies however do this for a living, full-time. They can invest enormous amounts of time and know-how, (and therefore money), into this task. An average Service Provider might have 3,000 solutions in that portfolio of Interims – all looking for problems to solve! So a busy HR Director might well feel that a meeting with that account executive is likely to be a better use of his time than a meeting with you.

SERVICE PROVIDERS CAN ADD VALUE. They are often very experienced executives in their own right, with deep understanding too of what an Interim Manager can be expected to achieve. So often the client will be persuaded to modify or redefine a brief, leading to a better assignment and a more satisfactory result all round.

SELLING TIME IS UNPAID TIME. Many effective Interims are plagued by those gaps – they have a wonderful daily rate when they are working, but the annualised outcome is severely cut back by those gaps between jobs. There never seems to be enough time, when you are working, to be finding that next job. Somehow getting work turns out to be a full-time job.

SELLING IS HARD WORK. Or embarrassing, or unpleasant, or demeaning, or not natural. If you find this at all true for yourself, then having someone else do it for you is well worth the discount.

Summary of Chapter 10: Inside an IM Service Provider

1. Service Providers are *marketing* businesses – they market *themselves* as useful intermediaries, *not* you personally.

2. Different agencies will vary their entry criteria from time to time. Find out – it only takes a telephone call.
3. Do not, as a beginner, venture beyond the membership of the IMA.
4. Being allowed to register just means that they feel you might be an appropriate candidate *if* they get an assignment which is a close fit for your niche.
5. Complete the registration fully and carefully. You have a lot of competitors out there. Make sure your CV spells out all your skills and achievements. You **must** be committed to self-employment.
6. Review, revise and re-enter your CV every 6 months.
7. A call from a Service Provider usually means that a search is under way. If you get an interview, use it as your chance to get 'coaching' for the sales meeting.
8. Always know the lowest daily rate you will offer the Service Provider for a typical 80-day assignment. Negotiate with that in mind when the chance comes. Listen carefully to any comments.
9. Service Providers generally work hard for their share – 20–35% of the rate billed to the client – and are better equipped to get business from big companies. Most Interim Managers are comfortable with a mix of direct and indirect business.

(11) *Doing the work – the easiest part?*

Don't worry, I'm not about to hand out instant guidance on how to be a finance director or a general manager, a head of manufacturing or a company secretary. Most times, as an Interim, you will be operating *at a level below* the highest level to which you were promoted during your employed career. See Chapters 10 and 12 for the reasons for this – principally it's the requirement that you be able to grip the assignment and start performing rapidly, without the luxury of a learning-curve. So the professional demands of most assignments might be expected to be interesting, even challenging sometimes, but not overwhelming – because you will have been there or thereabouts before.

What is important though is that you have a clear understanding of **6 WAYS IN WHICH AN INTERIM MANAGEMENT ASSIGNMENT DIFFERS FROM EMPLOYMENT**:

1. Be aware of the time-frame.
2. Focus on what is deliverable.
3. Identify who will be supplying that reference.
4. Be alert to the politics.
5. Build your internal network – quickly.
6. Getting paid requires special attention.

Of course, all of the above are significant in an employed situation as well. For example, TIME MANAGEMENT is always important to the busy executive. But somehow the special pressures of an interim assignment bring this issue into so much sharper focus.

Let's suppose you've landed, through a Service Provider, the assignment as Project Manager to relocate a manufacturing unit into a larger factory a few miles away, recently acquired by the company. It's a task you have successfully accomplished before, when you were employed. How can you ensure success again?

START WITH A 360-DEGREE COMMUNICATION PLAN – upwards, sideways and downwards. It's a fact of life that most of us are naturally more effective at communicating in *one or two* of the three dimensions – upwards to the boss, sideways to one's functional colleagues, downwards to the team and the people feeding into the team. Unless you were particularly unlucky, you would probably have found that, when you were an *employed* manager, the typical organisation would have evolved subtly around you, (more or less) to make up for any deficiencies you might have had as a communicator. But as an Interim, you don't have the time to wait on evolution! So make a plan and *a conscious effort* from the very beginning. Set out a communication programme – perhaps known only to yourself – to ensure that you have worked out who should be included in your network, and when, and how. Start with:

THE BOSS – most assignments actually have more than one! In the case of our Project Management task for example, there might be a Director of Operations, with line responsibility for the result. But the MD will certainly be interested, as will the FD, and the HR Director who might have made the original recommendation to use Interim Management. Sometimes it can be hard to tell who is 'the boss'. But your interest is in the result, not in corporate hierarchies. So for you the questions are, 'Who is going to sign off the job?', 'Who will provide my reference?' Then, *Render to Caesar*!

Two important steps – to be accomplished during the first 48 hours if at all possible:

1. REVIEW THE TARGETS FOR THE JOB. You had a brief from the Service Provider – check it over with 'the boss' – several 'bosses' if necessary – and establish how your progress will be monitored and measured and by whom. Write a little minute of this plan and send it to all concerned 'for comment and correction.'
2. SET UP A REPORTING ROUTINE – this could be no more than a promise of a short telephone call every Friday afternoon – but it could also involve a monthly presentation, or report to the Executive Board! Don't leave this routine to chance, whatever it is to be. Get it set up and diarised by all concerned. As a trade-off, ask the boss if he would like you to draft a note for circulation, explaining who you are and what your responsibilities will be.

Next steps:

1. LOOK FOR A QUICK GAIN – even if it's only a small one. You have a 'sponsor' somewhere, perhaps that HR Director, who has stuck his/her neck out to bring you on board, in the teeth of suspicion and opposition probably. So try to find – and make known – a quick payback to the company that will add enormously to the feeling that a good decision was made.

2. GET TO KNOW YOUR COLLEAGUES – people in different functions at more or less the same level as yourself, especially those reporting to 'the boss'. They are going to be naturally cautious, even suspicious at first. SO VISIT THEM as soon as possible, ideally just after the boss has put out that note about you. Offer them a one-minute potted biography, but don't be surprised if you don't get much in return – they don't have the same need for instant rapport. Explain what you will be doing, and a timescale if possible. Ask if there are ways you could be helping *them*, and be continuously on the look-out for signals of either support or anxiety. You do not yet know the local politics, nor where sensitive issues may lie. Remember that, compared with corporate timescales, most assignments do not last long enough for people to judge you entirely on performance. So you will need to help them to take as supportive a view as possible in the circumstances – i.e. tell them you know what you are doing!

3. BE A *LISTENER* ON YOUR OWN PATCH, especially with the people you will be managing or controlling. The project may look straightforward to you. But for the people who will have to live with it, there may be every kind of personal concern and doubt to be handled. So don't assume for a minute that they will be actually listening to what you say to them at the outset, especially if there are rumours of possible redundancies to come. Say as little as possible – ask questions that they have to answer, listen carefully, keep asking advice. Save the talking until you have roughed out a programme, and you then want their input into the detail. You might like to find opportunities to ask my favourite question:
'What one thing would make things go better for us?'

Being a stranger, and one who will not be figuring long-term in the corporate structure, can be a significant advantage. Many individuals will be delighted to use you as a sounding-box for their pet theory or programme. LISTEN EAGERLY. In every organisation, *there is always someone who has the right answer*. The problem comes when you have to decide which one is the one with that right answer, in that Tower of Babel . . .

Politics

To be avoided like the Black Death itself! The difficulty is in discerning which activities are 'legitimate attempts to assemble a weight of management opinion in favour of an appropriate move for the organisation', and which are distinctly less constructive.

A couple of real-life examples:

An IT start-up company, using an innovative technology, reached a promising position in its market. It then became progressively more obvious that the ongoing costs and time required to achieve adequate size and momentum were going to be significantly in excess of available cash resources. The company was certain to run out of cash. A solution emerged, when a large, well-established corporation offered to allow the fledgling to back its operations into its own, allowing a major part of the costs to be eliminated. However the consequence would be that the new company's technical and operations teams would be superfluous. The political manoeuvring that followed as alternatives were sought effectively paralysed the business, and eventually tore it apart.

The Financial Controller was an Interim, working a three-day week. In the series of sometimes ferocious discussions with the company's venture capital backers, every kind of pressure was exerted, every kind of inducement was offered to get him to come down on one side or the other. To his everlasting credit, he steadfastly remained even-handed. He produced the analyses that were asked for, and quietly pointed out what had *not* been asked for. He produced projections and forecasts, and drew polite attention to the assumptions behind the forecasts. In the outcome the business was sold on – but the Financial Controller continued to get a string of assignments from the venture capitalists. I guess he was very good at identifying which drum to march to!

In another example, a family company that provided a manufacturing service to the store-construction arms of the country's largest supermarkets had quadrupled its turnover – and *actually halved* its profits – over a five-year period. An Interim Manufacturing Manager was brought in 'to sort things out'.

The processes were not high-tech, but were complex in the way they had to be put together, and had to respond to *very* demanding customers. The problem was a familiar one to the Interim: this family company was still reliant on 'back of envelope' control systems, which had been adequate when the business was small, but which allowed horrendous bottlenecks to develop now the business had grown. Moreover each section of the process was under the control of long-serving supervisors, none of whom had an overview of the total business, and each of whom was personally committed to protecting his corner. Family owner/directors were actually in awe of these supervisors, and desperately reluctant to face up to the challenge of giving the Interim the authority he needed to put in and operate a planning system and then to help recruit an experienced manager to run the factory properly.

As a consequence the interim found himself between the Board who wanted control, but had neither the will nor the expertise to assert it, and the supervisors who refused point-blank to accept his leadership. The assignment was aborted – at least for a period. The Interim and the IM Service Provider were sharply reminded of a harsh truth – **an interim, no matter how talented, cannot succeed without genuine support from top management**.

Consultants, and interims working in quasi-consultancy roles are sometimes brought in deliberately to be used as sacrificial 'lightning conductors'. The Board in such cases probably knows perfectly well what needs to be done – but wants the cover of an 'impartial' outsider, to be the bearer of the grim tidings. The messenger gets the blame . . . but the decisions are 'regrettable but inevitable'. Occasionally the client will be open enough to spell out the anticipated scenario in advance – but rarely! More likely you will work it out for yourself. Can you avoid being loaded with the blame for an unpleasant outcome? Not easily. Perhaps the best advice is to seek an opportunity as soon as possible to discuss your likely findings *informally* with the top man. Tell him where you think you are heading, and ask for his support. You might get lucky . . .

Get that reference

Sometimes, in the early days of an assignment, it can be difficult to decide who it is who will be supplying your reference at the end. Don't be in too much of a hurry to decide . . . the saying is that, in any orchestra, there are half a dozen on the fiddle, another six just blowing penny whistles, but only one beating out the rhythm on the big base drum! Make sure you really understand who is setting the agenda, and tailor your reporting line accordingly. A busy executive might well respond favourably to your suggestion that you could save his valuable time by drafting the reference for him. If you get the chance, include as many specific numbers as possible to illustrate what you achieved – the boss can always strike them out if they are too confidential, (or too embarrassing.)

Extensions and cross-referrals

These are best discussed with your IM Service Provider, if you have one, as early as possible. Of course you would not be so unprofessional as to string out an assignment beyond its natural life. Ideally, establish timed targets early on, and take pride in demonstrating that they have been achieved.

It is perfectly proper to identify valuable extra work that you could take on, and to propose a contract extension accordingly. But don't be surprised if, perhaps through the Service Provider, you are invited to take a pay-cut. It's your decision – are they bluffing? Can you negotiate something in return?

Even more valuable may be a recommendation that gets you meetings with key executives of other divisions within a large corporation. Interims have used this technique to be able to operate for years within a big group. Those who don't ask usually don't get – so ask!

Working overseas

Quite a high proportion – 25–40% – of assignments are based overseas, most commonly in the overseas subsidiaries or associates of UK companies. There is seldom, if ever, a problem about foreign methods or systems for an Interim, for the simple reason that an Interim is only likely to be acceptable for an overseas posting if he's done something similar previously – you remember, 'been there, done that, got the scars to prove it!'.

So, as with most Interim assignments, the learning curve is very short and very steep. Generalising, the Interim needs to be 'culture competent' – i.e. at home and comfortable in the local environment. This kind of competence can only come from previous experience, say a minimum of a year or two in residence. Language skills are relevant too, of course, but the universality of English is such that empathy with the culture will be more valuable than total fluency in the language.

Practical points

Accommodation – should not be a big issue. The client should pay for accommodation of the same standard as would be provided for an *employed* manager of your status.

Travel – should be negotiated in advance, with some precision. Most corporations have established policies about standards of air-travel, Economy/Business/First. You will follow the same policy. For assignments in continental Europe, a typical arrangement is for the company to fund an Economy return air fare every second weekend.

The interim probably works through the middle weekend, but travels home on the second Thursday evening, being paid for a nine-day fortnight. More distant assignments – e.g. India, China and the Far East – are more demanding. It would be reasonable to propose:

Business-class travel
Good quality international hotel
Return on leave every three months for two weeks, (not paid, but free airfare).
Use of corporate doctors etc.

You do need to be careful though, when using the employer's facilities, not to compromise your 'self-employed' status. This is an especial concern if you are working direct, rather than through an IM Service Provider. It is tempting to pick up all the corporate support that's available. BE VERY CAREFUL! If you haven't done so recently, go to the Inland Revenue's web-site and read up as much as possible about IR35. If it is not obvious that you should be classed as self-employed, the tendency is for the Inland Revenue to class you as a Temporary Employee, with very awkward, quite expensive consequences for your 'employer', as well as for yourself.

Getting the money

It is a sad fact of business life, but sooner or later, unless you are very cautious or very lucky, you are going to come unstuck, and end up having worked hard for a month or two for nothing. That's £10,000 to £20,000 that you thought you had earned but will not receive. If the client company folds, your IM Service Provider should still pay you, since *they* are your creditor, not the client company. If you are working direct however, you have no such protection. You are just another in the long line-up of unsecured creditors, ranking behind the workforce, the bank, and the tax-men. You are not going to be safe even if you have personal control of the company's chequebook – make sure you understand the law relating to Fraudulent Preference; basically all unsecured creditors *must* be treated equally well, or equally badly.

So, how can you minimise the risk and/or limit the damage?

1. Take advice and take soundings. If you are a member, the Institute of Directors offers a by-return check of corporate credit-worthiness. On the job, if you do not actually have direct access to information about company cash-flow, keep a lookout for tell-tale

signs, such as suppliers not delivering until payment has cleared, or routine purchases having to be cleared by top management.

2. Invoice WEEKLY. If you have any doubts, negotiate payment in 7 or 14 days *ab initio*. Ask for an order number, which you include on every invoice.

3. Make friends with the Financial Controller. Explain that your weekly invoice is equivalent to your salary, so warrants being settled on contract terms.

4. Be punctilious about getting your time sheet signed off every Friday afternoon, together with your expenses. Hand in your invoice on Monday morning. Don't be shy about CHASING payment. Has your invoice been logged in? Has the boss signed it? When is the cheque run?

Mostly of course, your money is not seriously at risk. The company is solvent, you will get paid – but WHEN? Companies habitually pay suppliers on 60/90-day terms, and in the invoice clerk's office your invoice looks no different from any other. It's a bore, I know, but if you are working direct and you want to be paid regularly and promptly, you have to make the extra effort.

IM Service Providers can be helpful

Not just with getting paid! Their account executive will have negotiated the contract on your behalf. DO NOT HESITATE to give him/her a call regularly – say, once a fortnight – just to talk through how things are going, what has been achieved, what problems are coming up and so on.

YOU ARE NOT ALONE. On the contrary, there are several thousand active Interim Managers out there. In this chapter we have looked at the differences between being employed and being self-employed. You might now be interested to look in Appendix II, at some of the personal histories of Interim Managers, written by themselves, which will help to put flesh on the bones.

Summary of Chapter 11: Doing the work – the easiest part?

1. Be aware of the limited time available for you to achieve your objectives.

2. Develop and implement a 360-degree Communication plan.

3. Agree the deliverables and a timetable/routine of reporting. Identify a quick gain where possible.
4. Be alert and sensitive to the inevitable politics.
5. Establish who will provide your reference and set out to delight that person.
6. Look for additional work and especially cross-referrals.
7. Ensure that payment to you gets special treatment.
8. If an IM Service Provider is involved, pick their brains before, during and after the assignment.

Part Three

Mainly for Employers

(12) *Why use an Interim?*
(and how to find the right one)

If you are a potential or practicing Interim Manager, this section is not intended mainly for you, (though you will find it interesting.) This is intended *mainly for the employer*, who is considering the possibility of using an Interim for the first time. Particularly if you expect the idea to be challenged by the Board, say, and you need to be prepared with a reasoned analysis and justification.

Now hopefully you are in a position of some influence and power with a sizeable budget to control to help you to achieve your business objectives. So, why use an Interim Manager? Being the professionals we are, we would not dream of selling you 'Interim Management' in the abstract. That is only possible once we know your business, your needs, available budget and timescale. Besides that will be the task of the Service Provider or the individual Interim Manager. However there are a number of good general reasons for considering the use of an Interim which I think are well worth considering.

An Effective Strategic Resource

This has been mentioned before but bears repetition. Interim Management is a strategic resource to help you meet, not just your short-term needs but also your medium to long term skills shortages. Let us just think what that means. Suppose you have a business challenge which you cannot solve within your own resources. Within a week you can have identified someone *who has met a similar challenge in an industry similar to yours* and has brought it to a successful outcome. Well surely that is going to be hugely valuable?

'Wait', I hear you say, 'that is just the same old short-term-fix that Interim Management has always been associated with in the past? What's 'strategic' about that?'

Not so! Just because the placement has been made in a short timeframe, doesn't mean it is a short-term solution. You may have identified the requirement some time ago as part of you routine planning process. Perhaps you've cast your net widely internally, without finding the right skills. Or perhaps the skills are there, but no one will accept the challenge and risk a career. Then, having confidence in the Interim Management industry, you have put the requirement to the market place and your need has been met. So, not a just a quick fix, but a timely solution to a strategic requirement. Look at the case studies and profiles in Appendices I and II and see how IM's have been used to deliver real advantage.

Track record

Secondly an Interim Manager is an experienced and successful executive with a proven and demonstrable track record. When you take on an Interim you are getting someone who has been in a similar situation before and has brought it to a successful conclusion. To make this regulary possible, Interim Managers are inevitably 'sensibly over qualified.' This is the very opposite of the familiar Peter Principle, where executives are promoted to one step above their level of competence. Interims have, if you like, reached a plateau at which they feel comfortable and have widened their expertise at that level instead of trying to claw up to the next one. They are more than comfortable working 'one level down' – which *guarantees them the expertise to start performing instantly*. On starting an assignment, Interim Managers are always advised not to come with pre-conceived notions nor to try and apply a template solution to a particular problem, as some consultants might, but rather to use their experience of similar circumstances to achieve *your* desired business objectives.

Responsive

In a previous job I used to say that 'flexibility is the one principle that I adhere to rigidly'. Usually it got a laugh. But there is solid business case underlying it, especially in Interim Management. The service provided by Interim Managers must be flexible and responsive to the client's needs. Assignments are tailored to meet the requirements of the client, the objectives and, importantly, the budget. Assignments can be fulltime, part-time, defined as a project, be carried out on site or remotely or with any combination of these formats.

Sometimes an assignment may start off for 3 months but last 6 to 8 months, and vice versa. Most assignments start on 4–5 days a week basis but many taper off later. Interims will tend to like to keep a day a week in hand once the assignment is underway, for managing their own business, keeping their network alive and looking for the next assignment. But if the requirement is to work 6 or even 7 days a week then that is what will be done.

The service is responsive. Anyone who has used an interim will be able to tell you stories of placements made in 24 to 48 hours, although 7 to 10 working days is more normal. So a strategic resource which is *responsive to your need*, must be worth looking at.

Cost effective

The final major selling point is that Interim Management is very cost effective. That is *not* to say that it is cheap. It is not; but then neither is employing someone on a permanent basis. Few senior managers or directors, unless they are in HR, have any real idea as to how much it actually costs to employ a senior executive. Suffice it to say that without too much effort it is quite easy to show that senior personnel, even without bonuses or share options, can actually cost their organisation 50% more, and even up to twice their actual salary, (see the analysis in Chapter 8 Pricing). That in itself is quite alarming and when you take off holidays, training, sickness or other down-time and work out the number of days they actually work, (say 225 per year), it is easy to see that an interim even on £500 to £1000 a day can represent excellent value. In addition there are no on-costs, no terminal bonuses and no administration to worry about: just a simple monthly invoice from either the Service Provider or interim's own company. If you would like to consider more closely the economics of Interim Management, you will find our Chapter 8 on 'Pricing' very helpful.

Because Interim Managers are paid at a daily rate, the cost can easily be budgeted for and controlled. Indeed at the start of an assignment, the potential financial benefits of using an IM should be considered and compared with the anticipated costs. For some reason hard-headed business people, who would think very carefully about buying an expensive piece of equipment, will often consider taking on an Interim on a very casual analysis. Clearly the use of an Interim should be seen as an investment and appraised as such. If the benefits outweigh the costs then there is an obvious case for using this approach; if they do not, then maybe an alternative solution should be considered.

Possible problem areas

Clearly there will be a number of concerns over the use of an Interim Manager, especially for the first-time buyer.

Is it effective? A recent survey of UK managing directors of larger companies suggested that about 30% had used Interim Management. *And almost 90% were very pleased with the result and would use the service again.*

Cost is an obvious issue. I have already addressed this as a benefit but suffice it to say that for those working alongside an Interim the daily rate they are apparently receiving seems high. However in a similar way that employers do not realise the full cost of employing someone, employees do not understand the challenges of the independent career or lifestyle. You will have seen elsewhere that there is a lot that the Interim has to fund from their own pocket and the comparison with those still locked into a corporate career is a difficult one. The Interim has to provide value for money *each and every day* or their contract may be terminated. How many permanent employees are able to claim they do that?

The other major concerns focus around the issues related to bringing any outsider into a group or organisation.

- Will they be able to deliver?
- Will there be a good cultural fit?
- Will they be after my job?
- Will they take all our secrets to a competitor?
- Will they stay the course or be diverted by the offer of a 'real job'?

These fears can quite simply be allayed by remembering that Interim Managers are professionals who have chosen this career path of independence. They do not want a permanent job. They know that they are paid by results and are only *as good as their last assignment.* As Interim Management has become more established and better known, confidence in professional standards and ethics has increased. As true professionals the Interim Service Providers are joining the ranks of the other trusted advisers such as lawyers, auditors and, dare I say it, consultants.

How do I find one?

I have said in Chapter 3 that up to a third of all interim assignments are sourced through Service Providers. That of course means that two-thirds of all assignments are sourced by individuals direct to the client company or through other third parties who are not regular Service Providers. So since these represent the majority of assignments, let us look at those first.

Most Interim Managers, when they decide to make the break from corporate life, are advised to develop their own networks and refresh their recent contacts before striking out alone. So the chances are you might know someone yourself who works in this way and who just might be available. If you do, then talk to that person. This could well be your cheapest and quickest option and presumably you will know the ability of the individual you have approached. Just bear in mind that *choice and comparison usually improve the quality of a buying decision!*

Alternatively you might choose to network to one of your existing advisors and ask them it they know of anyone who might be suitable. Most professional bodies have registers of locums or stand-ins who are Interim Managers by any other name, and you might get lucky. The available data does suggest that is how most organisations have operated, initially at least. But if you are going outside your own experience for a solution, *it must make sense to at least talk to a specialist Interim Service Provider – talk is free!*

Service Providers

There are over 300 registered Service Providers who claim to be able to supply Interim Managers. Of those, just 10% are members of the Interim Management Association which is covered in more detail in Appendix III. If you are an employer considering the use of an Interim Manager for the first time, a member of the IMA has a lot to offer in the way of experience and good advice.

Service Providers have large data bases of Interim Managers, normally stored electronically, many of whom will have been interviewed before inclusion or registration. All will have been interviewed before being put forward on a short list for your consideration. Most serious Interim Managers will be registered with a number of Service Providers; typically 6 to 8 but sometimes a lot more. Service Providers tend to be either *horizontally* or *vertically* organised: 'horizontally' means that they will cover say 80% of job functions in 80% of the industry sectors,whilst 'vertically' implies that they will stick to one or 2 functions or sectors but cover a range of levels within that. Check their websites, see which ones operate in the area you are interested in and get to meet them.

If you accept the notion that Interim Management can be a *strategic* resource, then your relationship with the Service Provider will be a critical one. You will need to know that they are reputable, reliable and can meet your needs. You will also need to know the business processes they use and how much they are likely to charge you. I would suggest that for any business need or potential assignment you would be unlikely to want to deal with more than 3 providers and once you are happy with your relationship with them, the candidates they have provided and the results they have achieved, you may even narrow that down to one preferred supplier.

Assignment definition

If you are a first time buyer then before you even think about sourcing an Interim Manager you should clarify in your own mind your business objective and what you actually want to achieve. Ideally you should be able to quantify that and get a feel for the value of the benefits you expect to achieve from the use of an Interim. When you are happy that the potential benefits outweigh the actual costs then think about the sort of person you actually want to do the work.

Think how you want to define the assignment. Can you define it as a project with a start, a finish, desired outcomes and a resource allocation or will it need to be defined in more general terms? Can you identify milestones and timelines or must it be more flexible – if so how can you manage and control it? Having got these issues clear in your mind, if not actually down on paper, it is then time to approach the Service Providers you have identified as being ones you may want to work with.

You should remember that although it is often convenient to use a job specification from a permanent appointment, the skillsets required of an Interim can be significantly different. Interims are frequently brought in *to manage change or transition* which is a very different need from managing a steady state. Often an Interim needs to grasp only a part of the total job. So whilst the existing documentation may be a good starting point it is frequently only that. Discuss this freely with your Service Provider, and suggest that he drafts the task-specification for you. This allows him to input his experience of what Interims can achieve.

Candidate list

Reputable Interim Service Providers will want to come and visit you to discuss your requirements in detail and to identify how they hope to be able to meet them. This meeting is very important as they will be looking not just for the functional requirements of the assignment, but also for the softer skills that the successful candidate may require. Things like the culture and management style of the business, the reporting line(s), the degree of support or otherwise that can be expected. They will also need to work out with you some idea of the budget that will be required for the project. A Service Provider will often bring routine terms of business with them at this stage for your legal people to look through while they go away to compile their short list. The most usual areas to be queried are confidentiality, notice periods and payment terms.

Each company works in a different way but all will scan their data base electronically on any combination of job function, industry background, geography, price and keywords. From this they will compile a long list to be reduced to a short list once suitability, availability and rate have been confirmed. Most providers will then submit a list of, say, 3 candidates to you with their CVs, recommendations, costings and supported by referees if requested. This whole process can be completed if necessary within 2/3 working days so it is usually convenient to try to schedule times when the candidates will come to meetings at this first session.

Business meeting

Within 48 hours or so of the first meeting, you could be looking at the CV's of say 3 possible candidates from each of the Service Providers you have asked to work for you. From these you need to choose those whom you want to meet. Remember *these will be business meetings and not job interviews.*

Interviews are for permanent appointments, but these are business meetings – to establish whether the Interim Manager can convince you that he/she can meet your needs more fully, more effectively and more efficiently than any one else. The fact that they will be providing the service themselves does not matter, it should still be approached as a meeting of two company directors with the common aim of solving business problems.

The close

After you have had meetings with all the candidates you selected you should be in a position to choose one to undertake the assignment and to inform the Service Provider accordingly. You should then agree the rate, expenses and general parameters of the assignment confirming the overall objective.

Based on their terms of business, the Service Provider will then draw up a contract to provide the services of a nominated third party to work within your organisation for a specified rate for a given length of time. They will then have a mirror agreement with the Interim Manager's company. This is done to ensure that there is no suggestion that the interim is considered to be employed by either the client or the Service Provider. (Note: if your company contracts directly with the Interim, this issue needs very careful attention, ***especially in the light of the provisions of IR35).*** Once all that is done the assignment can begin.

Finally, after a hectic few days, pour yourself a glass of something refreshing, relax and enjoy yourself, you are in good hands! In the next chapter we will look at how to manage the Interim through the assignment and afterwards.

Summary of Chapter 12: Why use an Interim Manager? (and how to find the right one)

1. Interim managers bring experience and a proven track record of success to each assignment.
2. The service is flexible and responsive with some Interims being made available in 24 to 48 hours – although 7 to 10 days is more usual.
3. Although not cheap, Interim Management is highly cost-effective and should form part of a cost-benefit analysis.
4. There are a number of questions normally asked by the first-time user of Interim Management. Most can be readily answered as the professional standards of the industry become more widely understood and accepted.
5. Established Service Providers are most likely to be able to provide the consistent supply of high quality Interim Managers necessary for a strategic resource.
6. The job description and person specification for a permanent appointment may not always be appropriate for a similar Interim assignment.
7. The successful candidate will be selected as the result of a business meeting and not an interview.
8. The contracts framework between the client, Service Provider and Interim is formalised to ensure that *no employer/employee relationship can exist.*

13 Managing an Interim Manager
(and the legacy of the assignment)

Interim Managers are experienced, successful self motivators who are going to add value to your organisation. However they, and the assignment, need to be managed like any other business process to achieve maximum value. On the face of it, it is all pretty simple. Sensible, highly motivated professionals working together with your own managers, to achieve a common aim. But let us look at seven simple rules that will increase the chance of a successful assignment and a lasting legacy.

1. Assignment definition

We considered the assignment definition in general terms in the previous chapter when thinking about the requirement for an Interim Manager, but now we are going a bit further. I believe that it is essential to have clear and well defined business objectives for the assignment. For preference these should be written down, with timelines, and agreed to at the beginning of the assignment. If you feel you do not have the knowledge or skills to do this yourself, then the first week of the assignment could well be used to get the Interim to use his/her experience and expertise to recommend to you how it should be approached. But, at the end of the process, however it is done, at least the client and the individual should be able to agree what needs to be achieved and that the necessary resources are available to make it happen. It is often helpful to involve the Service Provider at this stage as well, if they have been used for the placement.

2. Buy-in

There are many reasons for bringing in an Interim Manager and it has to be admitted that some are less positive than others. When Interim Management was seen as a 'distress' purchase or purely as a means of managing a gap, this was often associated with a sense of failure and an awareness that the in-house team was unable to cope. But now there is a growing acceptance that the identification of a suitable opportunity, which can be met by bringing outside expertise, is a sign of strong, not weak management. Frequently too the in-house team know that there are modern methods or techniques which could improve their performance, so the arrival of someone bringing that expertise should be welcomed. Consequently it is essential that the management team and, when appropriate, the work force, whole-heartedly support the decision to invest in an Interim Manager and that their arrival should be presented positively. It should also be made clear, from the outset, the level at which the IM is working, to whom they are reporting, who is working with or for them and an outline of what is expected to be achieved. In my experience only once has the client *not* told the work force that the new manager was only there on an Interim basis (and it was then no surprise when the company went into liquidation the following year).

3. Joint venture, joint responsibility

I have mentioned this before but I think this notion of a joint venture is an important one especially if there is a Service Provider involved. It starts with the initial terms of business which will normally be presented at or soon after the first meeting. Once the assignment is agreed, the Service Provider will draw up contracts with the client and with the Interim Manager. This is done to help ensure that there is no suggestion that the individual is employed by either the client or the Service Provider. Although it is not my wish to discuss specific UK legislation here, it should be noted that although the contracts seek to establish the employment relationship, because the Interim is actually employed by his own company, they are not drawn up necessarily to give the individual exemption from IR35.

Once the assignment starts then your contact within the Service Provider will almost certainly want to come regularly to visit you both on site, individually or together, to make sure that everyone's expectations are being met. This can be seen as a bit of a chore but to my mind should be encouraged or even insisted upon. This is not just a self-congratulatory, business development opportunity with the possibility of a free lunch, but a chance to strengthen the relationship between all three parties *and to enhance the success of the assignment.*

Some Service Providers have specific sector expertise and your contact may well have been an Interim once, so they are able to offer specialist advice in their own right. Others are moving towards the common Dutch practice of securing, at their own expense, the services of a mentor for the Interim Manager for the duration of the assignment. Either way, the important point is that this is not a 'hire and forget' arrangement as found in other business sectors, but a close working relationship for the duration of the assignment and beyond.

4. Routine reviews

Clear and agreed objectives are an essential starting point for a successful assignment and so are regular reviews. Reviews can be formal or informal, recorded or not, but either way they are an essential part of managing the assignment. This is particularly important if the assignment is likely to move outside the original agreed parameters. Now that may seem a rather complicated way of saying that it is all going wrong! Agreed, but in my experience that is rarely the case. More likely is that the assignment is going too well and the interim has met the agreed targets too quickly!

5. Mission creep

Allied to the last point is the problem of mission creep. Interim managers are professional, dedicated and hard working. They are results-focused and enjoy a challenge; that is why many of them started in the first place. One inevitable consequence of this is that they are prone to taking on more work than originally agreed and that the job they end up doing is a long way from that originally specified. This may not be a problem but it does need to be managed.

Sometimes things change so much that the rate has to be reviewed and the contact re-negotiated, but more frequently the contract is just extended way beyond the initial period. Again this may not be a problem but remember why interims came into this field in the first place: variety, challenge, no corporate politics and a focus on results. Keeping them going and tying them with golden handcuffs may make sense from your point of view but there will come a time when they will want to move on and that also needs to be managed. A useful control is the *notice period.* Typically the contract states something along the lines of "100 days and thereafter subject to 20 working days notice on either side." This means that you should diarise DAY 80 as the first day on which to consider winding up the assignment. After that it will continue day to day, with 20 days notice in hand.

6. No-fuss Finish

One of the advantages of using an Interim is the availability of a clean break once the original, or subsequent, objectives have been achieved. This is normally thought of in terms of financial and administrative procedures, but in operational terms it is somewhat less straightforward. As the end of the assignment approaches the Interim Manager will start to have half an eye open for the next opportunity – or be gearing up for a well deserved break! However from your perspective the succession has to be planned and a smooth transition effected.

One useful way of doing this is to taper the assignment towards the end and encourage your Interim to do the last month's work over 2 months. He might work 3 days a week for the next month, 2 days a week for the second and then leave gracefully.

Many assignments end with the Interim being a useful part of the process to identify, recruit and induce the full-time replacement. This can lead to a mentoring relationship and on occasions even to a non-executive directorship. However it must remain a positive aspect of the assignment and the company or organisation should not be reliant on external assistance for ever. And so to the final challenge . . .

7. Managing the legacy

There are some who would argue that if an assignment does not involve managing change then it cannot be said to be a true Interim assignment. I would actually go one step further and say that all good management involves change or transition. You *manage* change but *administer* steady state. Therefore without changing the original definition, I think it is entirely reasonable to say that almost all Interim assignments will involve change, transition or business transformation.

Thus at the end of the assignment the challenge is to protect the substantial investment you have made in an Interim Manager and ensure that the changes made really are embedded into the culture of your organisation. Thinking about how to do this led me to a rather interesting paradox which in some ways brings us full circle.

I started off by defining Interim Management and then showing how the service can add value to an organisation and how it should be considered as a strategic resource. I hope we have shown too what sorts of people want to operate in this way, and why. Now here comes the paradox. Despite the fact that many Interims manage change and transition, *embedding that change requires a very different skills set.* Perhaps during the notice period, you should find time to review with the

Interim what his 'Legacy' will be, and, assuming it is wanted, work out who will be the 'inheritors', and how that legacy can best be embedded.

Interim Managers enjoy the excitement, the challenge, variety and freedom that the lifestyle offers. But to realise fully the results of their work, to embed a new culture or way of working requires a longer-term, more deliberate, and more measured approach by corporate man or woman. It is unfortunate that in some ways Interim Managers are seen as being higher profile and sexier than their corporately-employed counterparts, but a successful organisation will try to make best use of both. I like to compare then with runners. Sprinters are high-energy, high-protein, even high-profile. But who watches all of a marathon? Long-distance runners are less exciting, less charismatic even, but they are still considerable athletes

That is perhaps all I need to say to end. Interim Management is a high value, high achieving strategic business resource which can offer great and cost-effective benefits to companies and organisations in the private, public and not-for-profit sectors. But at the end of the assignment it needs the in-place, in-house team to accept the work that has been done and the contribution that has been made, and then to bring about lasting change in order to meet the business's longer term objectives.

Summary of Chapter 13: Managing the Interim Manager (and the legacy of the assignment)

1. An Interim Management assignment is a business process which needs to be managed like any other if it is to be a success.
2. It is essential that the requirements and expectations of all parties are fully identified at the beginning.
3. The assignment is a Joint Venture between the individual and the client company. The Service Provider too can have a role to play in bringing about a successful conclusion.
4. One of the great benefits of using an Interim Manager is a no-fuss finish; but this aspect of the assignment needs to managed and controlled as carefully as the rest of the assignment if the work done is to *fully embedded* within the organisation to produce a lasting and sustainable legacy.

Appendices

I Assignment briefs, candidates, outcomes – and reflections

In this section we move on from the piecemeal consideration of Interim Management and as it were take a bird's eye view of the battlefield – real live Interim Management activities. In each instance we will look at:

- The agreed Assignment brief
- Background to the chosen Candidate
- Summary of the Outcomes

We owe an especial debt to Mike Chapman, a senior personnel executive in a client company, who researched one of the outcomes of the assignments that feature in this chapter. His contribution is marked – *(MC)*.

Assignment No. 1 – Raise purchasing to board-level significance

The brief

Background: This manufacturer of critically-engineered components has as its customers the major manufacturers of aero engines. A year previously the company took over a significant competitor, and was in the process of consolidating operations onto its own site, where about 1000 will be employed, with sales of £60 million.

The job: Following the takeover, it was decided that the profile and significance of the Purchasing function should be raised, and a Head of Purchasing should be recruited. Reporting directly to the Managing Director, the person responsible will be responsible for approximately £30 million purchase of goods and services, with a department of 16. The task will be to develop partnerships in the modern style, always with absolute quality assurance.

Anticipating that finding the right person could take 6 months +, an Interim manager was proposed, to make urgent progress in this strategic task.

Parameters for selection:

1. *Experienced Mechanical Engineer*
2. *Top-level Purchase Management experience in a comparable business*
3. *IT literate.*

The Interim chosen

David Reeves was in his early 50s, a graduate in Economics who trained as a buyer with Ford, before progressing into senior management with Black and Decker and Johnson & Johnson. During this latter job he took a Diploma in Management Studies, (in his spare time!). He joined GEC Hotpoint as Purchasing Agent, was promoted to Purchasing Director, and became Product Director before moving sideways into GEC-Redring as MD. He was later Commercial Director of Russell-Hobbs-Tower, before his last job before independence, as MD of Spong Houseware. He had been an Interim for 4 years before this assignment came up.

The outcome (MC)

'During a period of business restructuring which included a review of Purchasing, an Interim was brought in as Head of Function to provide strong day-to-day management of the activity while keeping options open as to future organisation. This provided valuable breathing-space, giving time to assess the alternative scenarios – it would have been all too easy to rush into the wrong course of action. The Interim was able to bring his wisdom to bear in seeking to move to a more strategic sourcing structure, drawing on his wider base of experience, and exercising real independence of judgement. His methodology and structure were recognised as a model for other divisions within the group to study.'

Assignment No. 2 – Fill the HR Director's shoes

The brief

The company employed 800 in the UK. Its business is the selling and producing of advertisements for a large number of local trade directories. The environment is aggressive, fast-moving, results-oriented, and dominated by the pressure for sales performance.

The HR Director is being seconded into a corporate development activity on the Continent, and needed to hand over his critical UK role within three weeks at the latest. An Interim HR Director was an obvious solution. No immediate successor to the Director is apparent, and none should be needed. A re-organisation of the HR Department, (to be implemented by the Interim), will produce three HR line managers with regional responsibilities, getting rid of the previous hierarchical structure, and placing full responsibility at regional business unit level. There is a strong training culture in the company, and Training and Management Development functions report to the HR Director.

The requirements

An Interim on initially a six-month contract, with flexibility to extend. Reporting to the UK Managing Director, and with 'dotted-line' reporting to the Director of Administration in Brussels HQ. There is continuous pressure to recruit, train and motivate field and telesales staff in particular. Operating line managers are highly driven, but need firm guidance and support on matters affecting employer/employee relationships.

A strong, lively HR professional with a 'can-do' personality is needed, ideally from a retail/services background. There will be considerable freedom to develop policy, within business-plan limitations.

The Interim

Deanne Lee, in her mid-thirties, graduated with a BSc in Management Science. She trained in personnel with a local authority, then progressed rapidly through Philips, Shell UK, Mecca Leisure and Storehouse, where she was HR Director at Richard Shops. This was her first Interim assignment.

The Outcome

Deanne made an immediately favourable impression with her energy and professional skills. Her experience of recruiting and managing retail staff proved to be especially valuable, and helped the company achieve a sharp reduction in its historically high and expensive level of staff turnover. Sales staff were selected against tighter criteria, and effectively trained and motivated, so that they stayed longer and achieved more. The incumbent HR Director in fact did not return, so Deanne's assignment continued for 18 months.

Assignment No. 3. Establish best practice in a new business

The brief

A market for the sophisticated, controlled disposal of hospital and surgical waste was created initially by the Environmental Protection Act, and reinforced by EU directives. Previously, individual hospitals ran small, low-tech incinerators for this purpose, and these were now becoming non-viable. The company is a major diversified utility, which is developing a chain of specialised high-tech incinerators for this specific task, and expects to win a major (£20 million +) market share in a short time. They already have several hundred actual and potential customers.

To date, the incinerators have been developed and staffed in-house. Managers bring a strong understanding of incineration technology, but lack general experience of the wider field of operational management, and techniques for optimising efficiencies. The most important aspect of performance, from the client's and the customers' viewpoint, is the management of the collection service, against the time-critical operation of continuous batch incineration. There is a high level of complaints that either waste was not collected to schedule, or there were no available containers. An Interim Operations manager is therefore required, who, over a four to six month period,

(a) Will examine existing arrangements for collection, handling and incineration, for comprehensiveness and robustness.
(b) Will propose, introduce, modify, develop and test new systems.

The Interim

Ben Alexander had been a self-employed Interim Manager-cum-Consultant for 17 years, and had completed over 100 assignments. And he was still only just 50! Intellectually very bright, he maintains a fine ability to communicate on the shop-floor as well as the boardroom, and his enthusiasm is almost irresistible. The client was attracted by his very wide experience of dozens of different types of operations, his obvious delight in both learning something new and passing on his skills, and the fact that he is determined, committed, and prepared to shoulder responsibility.

The outcome

Over just a few weeks, Ben was able to model the business on his own laptop, and develop a series of well-tested improvements in method for every stage of the operation. The new Division was set up with enhanced effectiveness and improved customer image, to be expanded from four to nine incinerators over the next 12 months. In this example, an Interim Manager, by making himself a working part of the operational team, was accepted readily into the culture, and able simultaneously to manage the team, mentor his colleagues, and eventually produce a smooth handover.

Assignment No. 4 – Going Dutch

Background

The client is an old-established supplier of office administration systems; £100 million sales and 1,300 employees. In recent years it has developed strongly into computer systems, and has identified a specialised niche in services to motor distributors, (both vehicles and parts), where it is a major supplier with euro-wide ambitions.

The project

The company has just completed negotiations for an acquisition in Holland, which will be the start of a strategic move into the Continent. As a vital part of the process of integration, it is envisaged that an Interim Finance Manager will be needed for a period of 3–4 months, (not necessarily continuously).

Objectives

1. To establish an accurate financial position, and lay down a firm control system.
2. To introduce management control systems, fully compatible with those of the parent company.
3. To find/recruit/mentor in a Dutch successor.

Parameters

Qualified (ideally FCA) FD-level UK accountant, with competent Dutch language skills and experience of financial management in Holland. Strong IT skills and hands-on experience of divisional/branch management.

The Interim

Ches Clifton was in his late fifties, with a reassuringly avuncular style. His professional career included a period as General Manager of Coopers & Lybrand, Rotterdam, (and his fluent Dutch has been helped by his having a Dutch wife). His commercial career began in Trust Houses Forte, and after a move to Grand Metropolitan he became Finance Director of Mecca Bookmakers, and later MD of the international division of William Hill, Bookmakers.

The outcome

Ches was 'sensibly overqualified' for the job, and so was able to get respect and support without difficulty. His feel for the culture of Dutch business was as important as his language skills in helping to bed in the acquisition. The client was able to progress quickly, importantly without the need to depend on the former owners. UK-style reporting was rapidly established, and a Dutch Financial Controller (at a much junior level than Ches), was recruited, trained and left in charge. All within 4 months.

Assignment No. 5 – Going East

The brief

The client, a global multi-national manufacturer of engineered products, recognised that Indonesia would be a key player in future Pacific Rim developments. But it was short of the skilled management resources required to devote to the lengthy negotiation and start-up processes inherent in a joint venture, due to heavy commitments elsewhere in Asia. The task was defined as follows:

1. The structure to be a formal strategic alliance or joint venture between two or more partners, with a strong preference for equity control and management control by the client.

The methodology to be followed will include:

- An in-depth study and analysis of market opportunities for an Indonesian-based manufacturing facility.
- A search and review of possible local partners.
- Liaison with client business directors to incorporate their requirements.
- Preparation and presentation of a full strategic business plan.

The Interim

Mike Sanderson was in his early fifties, with a BSc (Mech. Eng.) from Durham, and an MBA from Wharton. His career has majored in Sales and Marketing, starting at Holman, then with Hyster (France and Africa) and Eaton Corporation (materials handling, Africa, USA and Switzerland). Then he became Marketing Director at Sykes Pumps, where his achievements included negotiating a JV in Singapore, and a technology transfer deal in Indonesia. Later he was GM at Wormor, and MD at Tirfor before going independent in 1991. He is one of the acknowledged 'stars' of Interim Management – skilful, professional, very determined, and a fine negotiator.

The Outcome

Unsolicited letters of appreciation are not common for Interim Managers; a letter as enthusiastic as this one is probably unique!

Just a brief note to express hearty thanks for the provision of Mike Sanderson to help set up our Indonesian joint venture in Bandung.

May I also express my unbounded admiration for the way Mike tackled the task in hand. First of all, of course, he had to understand the strange workings of our group which was no mean feat, but he took all that in his stride! Then he rapidly achieved total grasp of a very complex and ambitious project in Indonesia, the fragile but growing relationship with our partners, and all the necessary cultural sensitivities that one needs to observe when operating in Indonesia.

During the first engagement with us he thoroughly researched the market prospects and produced a most creditable business plan, which sailed through the Board sanctions procedure.

Having been engaged initially to produce this JV business plan, he then found himself during his second period with us acting as General Manager! Again, I was most impressed by his performance, enthusiasm and attention to detail with which he implemented the plan. In four months we saw astonishing progress as he created a business, fully fitted-out the factory space, and then patiently briefed the General Manager (when we found one) and handed over a virtually going concern.

On a personal level, he was always a pleasure to work with, and never lost his sense of humour, even when struggling to fight through the enormous quantities of red tape in the Indonesian Government approval process. We shall miss him!

Summary reflections

Five examples of Job brief + Interim manager + Outcome do not make a big data-base to support analysis and generalisations. But I hope you will take my word for it that if the data-base was 15 or 50 case-studies, the conclusions would not be very different:

1. The Interim that lands the job is likely to be substantially 'heavier' than the job would command as an employee. An exception would perhaps be Deanne's case – though even there her extensive 'frontline' retail experience gave the company a professional edge it had not had before.

2. Along with this apparent over qualification (in reality just the extra skill and experience essential to be able to get going instantly) goes the very close fit between the specification of the job and the experience of the Interim selected. Head-hunters will often be very creative in their choice of the shortlist, because a client can be persuaded to invest in *quality*, and allow for a learning curve. This seldom happens in Interim Management, because the need for instant performance is too pressing to allow it. Hence my advice that you identify yourself strongly with your niche, broadening it only as the accidents of experience allow you to claim a right to more territory.

3. Of course my five outcomes were all successes: I believe success follows a pattern, (whereas the occasional disaster is unpredictable). Apart from the qualities and experience of the Interim manager, the other principal component of success is *an agreed and sensible (in the timescale), set of objectives*. An Interim can be very focussed, in a way that an employed executive often cannot be. He can use his wider knowledge to propose appropriate, achievable outcomes without any element of bravado or 'stretch'. Afterwards, good communicating techniques leave the client with a warm feeling of confidence, and of money well spent. Which is what good marketing aims to achieve, isn't it?

II Real live Interim Managers

The following profiles are written by successful and practicing Interim Managers. They were asked to give a brief life history, the reasons for becoming an Interim Manager, their likes and dislikes and to outline a favourite assignment.

The picture that emerges from this is of great interest. Firstly there are many similarities in their backgrounds and reasons for coming into Interim Management. Secondly there are a number of common themes which account for their likes and dislikes of the business and lifestyle. Finally there are the very positive conclusions justifying if not the decision to come into Interim Management, at least the reasons for staying.

These profiles are very much in the words of the Interim Manager and have not been editorialised other that to give a measure of consistency of style and layout. What emerges is a fascinating account of the life and works of real Interim Managers written by the people who should know it best.

Howard Wyer-Roberts

1. Life history

Howard is a graduate microbiologist with an initial career in the food industry.

His early career was spent with Cadbury Ltd and Grand Met where he progressed through marketing, sales and distribution eventually becoming MD of Europe's largest Foodservice organisation. He has also occupied positions as Buying Director for Fine Fare Supermarkets and Managing Director UK for Ireland's largest dairy products company.

Howard joined PA Consulting Group and with a small team pioneered the introduction of Total Quality Management in the late 1980s and early 1990s.

He has successively been a partner in a consultancy and recruitment service organisation and latterly a director in Manor House Consulting Ltd providing consultancy and Interim Management solutions.

He has carried out successful projects for large and small organisations and has worked in both the private and public sectors and is currently undertaking a business strategy and change programme for a plc in the Logistics industry .

2. Why IM?

Howard entered IM by accident rather than design. A phone call from a head hunter suggested a role that might be available to someone who viewed the position flexibly. In practice this job became an Interim role. Subsequently, registration with a variety of IM Service Providers triggered prospective Interim roles.

Being already used to short/medium term assignments as a management consultant, the prospect of Interim work was really 'more of the same'. The regular change of scene and new challenges still provide the biggest attraction coupled with the ability to plan one's business life and personal life more flexibly.

Incidentally the first assignment was tedious, frustrating and not intellectually rewarding. But there is always the next assignment!

3. Likes and dislikes

Working is a necessity; firstly for economic reasons, secondly for personal fulfilment.

The good bits are:

1. Meeting and working with some excellent people.
2. Job satisfaction.
3. Knowing that there is a definite end to an assignment (usually) and being able to plan accordingly.
4. Fee rates are sometimes very good.

and the bad bits:

1. Feast and famine – sometimes having to turn away attractive jobs.
2. Occasionally having to stick something out even when you don't like it.
3. Not being able to see something through and realise the benefits.

Realistically even if you wanted to, returning to conventional employed status after the age of 50 is difficult. So Interim Management extends the useful working life.

4. Favourite assignment.

Hard to choose, most assignments have been enjoyable and of benefit to the client but the following one is of particular interest:

Project Change Executive, Acting Director of Strategy and Oversight –
'Motability'

Interim Management brief

Assist client in designing and implementing a change programme;
programme to comprise the outsourcing of major operational activities
and the re-structuring of the organisation. Operate as acting director
of the new directorate until the appointment of a new permanent
director.

Background

The client is actually the largest car leasing organisation in Europe with
400,000 customers. It is organisationally unique being part publicly
funded by government and part privately funded. The sourcing of
funds and the provision of vehicles is organised through a consortium
of UK banks. The client wished to pass over virtually all the
operational aspects to an outside Service Provider but in so doing put
in place performance control mechanisms. The client had already
retained a contact centre to deal with customer applications, approval
and authorisation.

This major change brought with it the need for:

1. An overall programme for change and the means of delivering it.
2. Design of a new directorate to oversee performance of external
   Service Providers as well as internal functions.
3. A set of 'heads of agreement' leading to a formal contract with the
   major Service Providers.
4. A culture change so that two key elements of the supply chain
   would work more harmoniously.

Achievements

1. Drew up and integrated the many project streams that were being
   pursued in an unstructured way within the business; produced clear
   overall programme with individual project sponsors and account-
   abilities.
2. Created and facilitated directors' steering group for managing the
   client programme, chaired project managers' progress meeting.
3. Produced new organisational design with new directorate responsible for managing strategy and development in addition to its
   responsibilities for overseeing the performance of the whole

organisation; designed performance management framework to support this new concept.

4. Designed process for the review of existing competencies of staff in relation to new requirements; designed process for staff development/external recruitment to fill organisational gaps.
5. Worked with company solicitors in the drawing up of 'heads of agreement' for major Service Provider.
6. Designed 'values audit' needed as a precursor to the planned culture change.

Later

To date, the main Service Provider has accepted the need for business process re-engineering of his operations and a 10% reduction in operating cost. This is a direct consequence of the new contractual negotiations and the intended performance measurement approach that is now being introduced. As a result of this assignment Howard won the 'Interim Manager of the Year – Change Management 2003'

5. Conclusion

IM is OK for some. IM suits me because of the flexibility. Best for the older executive, 45-plus where the family has grown up so don't miss father being away. For the younger ones with families the uncertainty of income will be a major negative.

Suits me fine – hope to go on working as long as clients are willing to use me.

Robin Taylor

1. Life history

With a first degree and a doctorate in chemistry, I found in my first role as a scientist that the people issues in the business were far more interesting than the technical ones. I thus embarked on a career in personnel beginning in the pharmaceutical industry where I could work in a relatively familiar environment while learning new skills. Part of that was through the professional body – the Institute of Personnel Management – going back to college.

Since then I have experienced Personnel or Human Resource management in a variety of sectors. The main driving force in making career moves was to build up a wide range of experience according to what was important at the time. The early days were focused on industrial relations in highly unionised industries and employment legislation, as the concept of employment protection began to develop.

Having headed the HR function for a period of time and handled tough IR issues, major start up recruitment, relocation and other changes I made a complete change. Reacting to the criticism of HR that it was not business focused, I spent 3 years at the customer interface in Retail. But HR was always my main interest and I returned to head the function in a number of different service businesses. In such organisations HR has to be commercially aware and immersed in the business. This exposed me to restructuring, downsizing and other major organisational changes.

After a year or two working on a consultancy basis, a situation precipitated by the recession of the early '90s I was keen to return to the corporate life and also to the life sciences field. That began a lengthy period in various parts of the pharmaceutical industry – where I began my career in HR.

My re-entry was into another service business providing clinical services to pharmaceutical and biotech companies. It was a fast growing, flexible, 'can do' and 'have to do' environment with a lot of pressure and few resources. Moreover it was a sector embracing a large number of consultants and self employed people.

During my 6 years there the 'have to do' feature meant for me, taking on a wholly new role in managing property and facilities in addition to HR. It gave me some high value and short deadline projects to manage, all critical to the business.

Taking stock of my career it appeared that I had built up a very wide range of experience in large and small organisations, single and multi site operations, UK, European and US owned companies, unionised and non-union businesses and a variety of sectors. But how much of this could I realistically draw on in corporate roles?

2. Why Interim Management?

I had considered consultancy and tried it out in a small way. I had experienced the use of consultants. None of this gave the buzz of carrying out and *achieving* things in a corporate role. Seeing consultants at work had convinced me that I would be unhappy not to be involved in the doing and never to see the real end product. Perhaps more importantly I could never see myself doing the same thing, albeit with some variations on a theme, for client after client.

Then I heard of the relatively new concept of 'Interim Management'. This was not for the analyst, blue skies dreamer, proposer and escapologist. The Interim Manager had to get moving fast, keep going and complete to deadline and budget and then move on to a quite different project calling on other past experiences for inspiration. It was a customer-facing role needing a 'can-do' attitude and flexibility. These were all characteristics of businesses I had worked in for quite some years and what I had enjoyed about them.

The Interim Manager does not have to be the corporate politician nor does he or she have to share the corporate values of the organisation – just avoid conflict with them. It would be an opportunity to think back over previous experiences, the good and the bad, the successful and less successful and conclude what might best suit the present circumstances – in short, *freedom.*

As the various constraints on life such as mortgages, dependent children and their education began to recede it seemed that Interim Management would offer freedom in other senses too – freedom to work in different locations, possibly abroad, this month but not during the high summer, for this client rather than that one.

So I finally decided to set out on a career in Interim Management. How? By the simple expedient of running through organisations *in the sectors I knew best.* I chose one with fairly obvious people issues, thought through what they might be, picked up the phone and suggested how I might help. I am now in my third Interim assignment with this organisation. Both previous contracts were extended twice.

3. Likes and dislikes

There is no doubt that the freedom I expected is there but it is also limited by the number of assignments available, my own availability and my suitability to undertake them. Certainly there is freedom in that one can try out new approaches and strategies, perhaps ones you chose not to adopt in similar circumstances before. While the role is quite different from that of a consultant, there is one similarity in that you should aim to meet the client's needs to get repeat business. So what you do needs to be credible and stand the test of time.

One of the major issues facing the Interim is the confusion between Interim Management and Consultancy. Also the word 'interim' has been hijacked by low-level employment agencies as the latest name for agency temp, (Especially in the USA, *editor*).

The subtle shifts in emphasis in employment/tax law regarding employment status have also had an impact in that we are all 'workers' now at least for many purposes. So the difference between employed status and an independent Interim or any other kind of short-term assignment is becoming wafer thin.

Having to run a limited company, which is mandatory when working through some of the most respectable Interim Providers, can be a chore. This is especially so when working with some clients and sectors who insist on employing short-term staff of any kind either on their own payroll or as self-employed workers. Such inflexibility can arise even when the client is very accustomed to using small limited companies in other functions such as IT or finance.

Marketing and networking to ensure a reasonably steady flow of assignments is a challenge especially when trying to focus on a demanding project that may consume a great deal of time. But one cannot depend on Interim Service Providers for many leads and down time is an inevitability. That can be very frustrating.

Then there are 'potential' clients. Many, it seems, reach for their list of Interim Providers before giving much thought to whether the work they have in mind might make an Interim assignment or even whether it exists at all. So 90% of potential Interim assignments probably either never get off the ground or become internally reallocated work.

But it is the freedoms, the self-control and the fact of doing a job and particular kinds of work that you enjoy that makes all of these irritations worth bearing.

4. Favourite assignment

My favourite assignment has to be my first with PRA International, not least because I had the opportunity of seeing at first hand where they were over 2 years later.

The presenting problems were these:

1. The client had very recently acquired a UK company but had little if any experience outside the US.
2. The acquisition had not been well received by a sizeable proportion of the staff and managers and attrition was very likely.
3. The client was in a high growth sector.
4. The company profile with customers and potential employees in the UK was very low.
5. The company had to relocate very soon after the acquisition.
6. Recruiting had to be at minimum cost.
7. There was little HR infrastructure.

The key client expectation was that a team would be recruited to replace those who left and so build a cohesive and effective contract research group.

My role was to undertake recruitment as cost effectively as possible and creatively to find high calibre staff. Also I had to coach and support a small and fairly inexperienced HR team, helping and advising them on employment law, UK best practice, policies and procedures, and the design of a handbook. It was also to coach managers in how to handle people issues effectively and positively.

I reduced the cost of recruitment by 50%, when compared with the past practice of using agencies, by advertising locally as far as possible, using networks and my own search to avoid cost altogether. Also I ensured that as many potential employees as possible were interviewed face to face so that, whether hired or not, they took away a positive impression of the organisation, its people, it values, recruitment processes and the office environment. Soon candidates were contacting us having heard of PRA from a friend or colleague.

I was approached by a recruitment consultancy that had received feedback from potential candidates they had contacted on the positive, professional and confidential way in which their dealings with PRA had been handled.

Having returned to PRA 2 years later, despite being forewarned that there had been a great many changes, I was surprise how many 'friends' I recognised. Also the team had grown considerably and matured significantly, partly because of my coaching. The training commitment was outstanding, being driven by one of my recruits. . Another recruit, hired by personal search, is now the UK Vice-President., and the organisation does not feel particularly American.

5. Conclusion

No regrets despite the frustrations. 'Going Interim' has given me more time for normal family life, a lot more flexibility and freedom than I ever had in the corporate world and I can choose the kind of work I like and that fits with my strengths and experience.

Alan Smith

1. Life history

I joined Birds Eye Foods from school and became a production planner. Moved into Industrial Engineering (Work Study in those days) and worked at various sites before being picked up on the management development program involving in-house General Management training, and then took on a Production Manager role.

Progressed through various other companies and roles through production management, and factory management to Operations Director.

From 1992 to 1997 Operations Director of Kitchen Range Foods, Huntingdon Cambs. This role involved the design, build and commissioning of a new factory on a greenfield site.

Moved to Grampian Convenience Foods (a division of Grampian Country Foods) as Operations Director for a short period before moving into IM and self-employment in 1998.

Professional qualifications: Member of Chartered Institute of Management, Member of Institute of Management Services, Member of the Institute of Interim Management.

2. Why IM?

My move into IM was made in July 1998.

Having made something of a career of changing jobs and employers, all in the food industry and latterly at the Operations Director/Production Director level, I found myself in a situation where I recognised that I had joined the wrong company. My management style and that of my new employer were not aligned and the only solution appeared to be to move on.

Having promised my family there would be no more house moves I looked at the options available other than simply trawling the jobs pages again. I had heard of IM and started to look further into what was involved; I even bought and read Dennis Russell's book. The appeal of self-employment started to grow as did the opportunity to enjoy a new situation every few months – the potential to work in new, different areas and meet new people was also attractive. The final decision to move into IM was made after attending a one day IM workshop run by ATIES (now IMA). After a very brief period in which I considered Consultancy, it was soon clear that IM was the route for me.

Having agreed an exit package with my employer (quite generous after only nine months' service) I left corporate employment and formed my limited company, produced a brochure, registered with most of the Interim Agencies in the ATIES listing and started to contact my many friends and previous colleagues in the food industry. It was a conscious decision to 'stick with knitting' and only approach food companies.

In just a few weeks my first assignment came via a previous colleague. This was a two week investigation into a process of post-pack pasteurisation for cooked meats and had to be carried out without reference to the client company. The report included options and factory layouts with budget capital costs.

This was my first (and last) taste of working from home in the true sense' as I only visited the client for initial briefing and then presentation of my report. An interesting experience and also useful as two years later I was asked back to the same company and stayed with them for ten months at two different locations.

3. Likes and dislikes

For me there are two main down-sides to the life of an Interim Manager:

Firstly no work, no pay.

Secondly the probability of spending considerable periods of time away from home.

Of my seven years as an IM, four and a half have involved working away from home from Monday to Friday weekly.

On the other hand . . .

The one common denominator is newness. Every new assignment begins with the thrill of the unexpected and the expectation of meeting new people, learning new processes, sharing experiences and expanding the network of friends and colleagues. It is also a chance to relate all of my 'when I was at so-and-so stories'.

Most assignments seem to end up lasting 10–12 months even those declared to be for say six to eight months. It seems that if the company/team like the way you work the role develops and the brief expands. Indeed it is often said in Interim circles that it can be more difficult to get out of a company than it was to get into it in in the first place!

The role of an IM is a rather special one and it is common to find yourself in possession of confidential, often very sensitive, information. As a visitor to the company the IM is often in the position of being a safe sounding board, and hence party to a company's plans or intentions at a very early stage. Clearly this brings with it a high level of responsibility and trust and the IM must never be in a position where his/her integrity is in doubt.

It is always pleasing, indeed flattering, when a client company asks if I would like to join them permanently – but I would not change this way of working and earning.

4. Favourite assignment

The glib answer to the question 'What has been you favourite assignment' is that the current one is the favourite because it is topical and has that much sought after newness.

However, of all the many and varied jobs over the last six years my favourite is probably the year spent with Swithenbank Foods in Bradford.

SFL (now owned by 3663) was a £25 million per annum turnover privately-owned company. The operation at Bradford supplied Food Service customers nationwide with a full range of fruit, veg and delicatessen products six days a week with orders taken on Day One delivered early on Day Two. Customers in the south of the country were serviced via a depot in New Covent Garden, London.

The company was in a difficult position in that it had decided to remove most of the senior management team at short notice and obviously needed to put a new team in place to maintain customer service and in effect keep the business alive.

The new MD, with whom I had worked in corporate life, pulled together a nucleus senior management team in advance of the changes and my part in this was as Interim General Manager. The other team members were existing employees from within the group.

This was the ultimate in hitting the ground running as there was no time to learn the ropes and no latitude to make too many mistakes. In the early critical days finding who in the remaining team could be trusted and relied upon was crucial, and this had to take place in a highly charged, rather tense atmosphere.

Main achievements were re-structuring and rebuilding the Operations team; installing efficiency measures including delivery performance, complaints indices and labour planning/control; reducing customer complaints.

Along the way we unfortunately lost the business of one major customer and it was necessary to make eighteen employees redundant.

The enjoyable aspects of this assignment included the large degree of freedom to identify needs and take action as appropriate; also the availability of funds for improvements where necessary and justifiable. It was also an enormous pleasure to be working with an enthusiastic team, all of whom shared the same goals.

This was my first experience of working with a largely Asian workforce and presented a huge learning experience along the way. The guys also made me very welcome and this is a great help in Interim Management.

The assignment concluded after eleven months with the recruitment of a permanent General Manager who, as it turned out, was a colleague from a previous Interim assignment.

5. Conclusion

It is often said that the one thing Interim Managers have in common is a low boredom threshold. I am proof positive of this. It is also said that Interims like to work for half the year and holiday for the rest. This is not my own approach but I would admit to taking generous holidays subject to the demands of the assignment at the time.

As a reward for spending long periods of time away from home I usually take off the whole of August to spend with the family as well as a full Christmas break.

However, the biggest buzz in being an Interim Manager is the opportunity to really make a difference in the client company while working with new people, learning new skills and earning a living. What more could a chap ask for?

As an Interim I can honestly say that I actually enjoy the job of work more than at any other time in my career.

Janet Morris

1. Life history

Following a degree in Business Studies, I joined BAA's excellent graduate training programme. This gave me experience in all aspects of airport management – operations; business planning; strategy; corporate and public affairs; and marketing. One of my most enjoyable roles was to work closely with the airlines, either existing or start up, to help them develop their routes at the three main London airports. During my time in this job, one of the most interesting things that occurred was the receiving of a fax from a Greek shipping magnate proposing to set up a low cost airline from Gatwick. My boss and I didn't take it seriously enough – and before we knew it Easyjet had launched from Luton Airport! Following this, I spent eighteen months as the 'right hand man' to Des Wilson, the renowned campaigner and self publicist during the 'Terminal Five' campaign. This gave me an excellent insight into corporate & public affairs as well as media relations. In 1995 I was promoted to become the Head of Marketing for London's Stansted airport – this was a fabulous job helping to sell the airport to both airlines and passengers. My final role at BAA was the Business Development Manager for the launch of Heathrow Express. I was responsible for everything at the Paddington end of the operation. During this time I completed an MBA, sponsored by BAA. I then decided to take voluntary redundancy to try pastures new; this led to me becoming an Interim Manager.

My experience as an Interim Manager has, so far, covered marketing roles with companies as diverse as airlines, law firms, a headhunter and a public sector organisation.

2. Why Interim Management?

During my twelve-year career at BAA I had been fast-tracked into a number of roles – the longest I spent in any role was eighteen months so I was used to being 'parachuted' into roles to manage projects. This gave me an ideal foundation for Interim Management and its generally short-term assignments. I had always wanted to work for myself rather than being part of a large corporation – this would enable me to show my true strengths and abilities. The biggest challenge was getting the first assignment. I was put forward by a specialist Interim Provider within the marketing sector. My first role was to integrate four recently merged logistics companies into one brand. Following a successful project I was asked to stay on to head up Sales, Marketing and Customer Services which I continued to do, on an Interim basis. From this assignment I have never looked back and have been able to move from assignment to assignment – with, so far, only one month's gap in the early days. I have now been an Interim Manager for six years and am currently on my twelfth assignment – three of which were concurrent on a part-time basis.

The night before my first assignment I remember reading marketing textbooks and being scared. But now I have so much experience from a number of roles in a variety of industry sectors. I have a great deal more knowledge, experience and confidence. It is great to be always learning as well as taking ideas from one industry sector to another.

3. Likes and dislikes

Interim Management has been excellent for me. I started at the age of 35, which is relatively young (the average age is getting younger, but still in the region of 50 – I would imagine). This has meant that I have been able to develop and gain experience whilst being an Interim Manager – meaning that I have been able to advance during this time. I have remained an Interim Manager, by choice, as I enjoy the flexibility and learning that it allows. On a number of occasions I have been offered permanent roles which I have chosen not to take.

The 'likes and dislikes' as I see them:

Likes

1. Flexibility for holidays/days off/working from home
2. Ability to learn different industry sectors and working styles
3. The bringing of ideas/experience from one industry to another
4. Having specific defined responsibilities/objectives and the ability to say "No – that is not my area".
5. Generally the ability to stay out of politics/gossip
6. Interim Managers are often used during a period of change – I enjoy working in a changing environment
7. Enables me to operate at a senior level due to the amount of experience I have obtained
8. Able to also do consultancy work in addition to the interim roles
9. The money is rewarding too

Dislikes

1. Sometimes feels as if I do not belong
2. Not involved on some occasions – as not a permanent employee

4. Favourite assignment

This must be my last assignment working as the Interim Director of Marketing for the Energy Saving Trust (EST) which was set up in 1992 following the Rio Summit to encourage individuals to reduce their energy use, to reduce carbon emissions and ultimately to reduce the onset of climate change. I joined when the Marketing Department had been centralised, from thirteen smaller teams, into a single team of thirty-seven people (seventeen of whom were temporary and contractors). The staff had been literally pulled together on an organisation chart! There were no systems or procedures to support them – the staff did not even know each other's names or responsibilities!

As EST is very Government programme-driven it has grown into 'silos'. The organisation had never had an overarching business or marketing strategy. The business strategy was delivered by one of my colleagues early in my assignment and one of my first tasks was to pull together an overall marketing strategy for the organisation. This made it very clear that the Marketing Department structure would be more efficient if it were organised by audience so that all of the relevant programmes could communicate to each audience in a joined-up and relevant manner. The department was restructured into a number of audience-focussed teams. This enabled the temporary staff and contractors to be offered permanent roles, leading to more stability for the department. In addition to structure, a number of other key areas were identified that needed sorting out – EST had seventeen websites; ten call centres; seven PR agencies; a number of databases; a poor profile in the media corporately etc. etc. etc. all making it expensive and time-consuming to manage.

My task was to develop the strategy for these areas and to oversee their implementation to ensure that the customer was at the heart of the organisation's thinking and that everything the organisation did was simple for people to understand and it was easy for them to take action in a cost-effective manner.

With all of these items working more effectively EST has now recruited a permanent Marketing Director to manage the ongoing department. His role is to continue to implement the plan I set up, and to maintain the status quo.

5. Conclusion

I believe that I am only half way through my career and that I will continue to develop, take more time off, earn more per day, and gain from the experience within different industry sectors. My dream is to work six months of the year and have six months off with my friends and family.

David Slee

1. Life history

My early years were spent on the move, with childhood in South and East Africa and later schooling and university in the UK. As a family we travelled between Africa and the UK and I therefore acquired an international interest at an early age. A degree in social sciences led to an interest in personnel work, confirmed by an industrial placement during my degree course in the personnel function of Rolls Royce in Derby.

Graduation led to a temporary role in sales and I soon learned that selling was not for me. I joined IBM in their personnel function, working initially in compensation and benefits. The significance of IBM for a first role in personnel (it was not yet called Human

Resources) was that the industrial relations climate was not like that in other large British companies. To this day, my experience of Trade Unions remains slight.

Seven years later a change of direction came about with a switch into consultancy and a move to Hong Kong and Singapore. Working for Hay I was part of a team providing a wide range of consultancy assignments to clients in a number of Far Eastern countries. It was a fascinating few years with amazing challenges, not least confirming an interest in working internationally. The consultancy role continued with my return to London, and for a number of years afterwards. The international flavour continued too; over half of my work was with companies based in Continental Europe.

By now, with a background in both personnel and consultancy, it was time to move back into a senior personnel role and I became European Director of Personnel for one of my clients and this became my first Interim role – in 1986. The company was made up of a number of subsidiaries, both wholly owned and joint ventures with a very lean head office structure. It was clear that there would be no place for a permanent Personnel Director, but there was plenty to do in creating the function and establishing good personnel practice in four main companies in over a dozen countries. We agreed a fixed term of two years.

When the role came to an end I had one last try at a permanent personnel role with the position of Personnel Director in the distribution industry. This too involved setting up and creating a function, with the additional role of Quality Director. However, it ended with redundancy after two years. Consultancy, self-employment and later, Interim Management became the obvious course of action.

2. Why IM?

Interim Management was not a conscious choice – in 1989 it did not really exist. The shock of redundancy necessitated a re-think and I was very lucky to have a number of contacts who ensured a steady stream of consultancy work. This was largely related to compensation and benefits, but also a range of other interesting projects, including carrying out training in Kuwait. However, this was not part of a plan for the rest of my career, it just happened. I was clear that I did not want a return to corporate life and I wanted to continue enjoying the wide variety of challenges that had been mine over the last few years.

The options therefore were either to join a consultancy or to work with a group of like-minded people in building our own consultancy business and for a number of years this was what I did. We were successful in gaining a number of interesting assignments.

Critical here was the variety of work, control over one's own destiny and the ability to achieve a better work/life balance. However, there was always the question of where the next assignment was coming from. We spent a lot of time building and marketing the business in addition to carrying out consultancy assignments. There was not always as much work as we would have liked.

The turning point was a telephone call from one of the then major Interim Management Service Providers suggesting an Interim assignment. The opportunity was an interesting one and was something I had done several times. Take an existing Personnel Department and turn it into something much more aligned to the objectives of the business. The client had a Personnel Manager who was leaving and while they were recruiting a Human Resources director they needed someone to start rebuilding the function.

Winning the assignment wasn't easy – it involved several interviews and a presentation to the Board. They liked what they heard and I began work. The establishment of the new function was successfully done and in due course the newly recruited director started work. The twist was that, instead of leaving and starting to look for the next assignment, they asked me to stay on in a completely different role. From being Interim Personnel Manager I became Interim Head of Operations in the security industry. Now, instead of managing a human resources function with five people, I had 400 engineers providing service to business and domestic clients throughout the United Kingdom. Challenging targets were set and met. My first experience of managing a large number of people had been a success.

The consultancy and the Interim lives ran in parallel for a while – we even achieved some success in supplying Interim Managers. However, for me it was clear, I preferred Interim Management to consultancy.

3. Likes and dislikes

There are many things about Interim Management that fall into the 'likes' category. They include control over one's own life, considerable variety, additional challenges and much higher earnings. The dislikes are fewer – the main one of which is the uncertainty of winning 'the next assignment' and a certain degree of uncertainty over earnings.

Control over one's own life means that you don't get called into your manager's office to hear that you are going to be made redundant. As an Interim Manager you <u>know</u> that you will eventually be told that your time is up, and you welcome it.

The variety and the additional challenges are what make it so rewarding. Every assignment is different; at least half of my assignments have started out in one area and ended up in another. From Personnel Manager to Head of Operations, from Human Resources Director to managing a merger between two banks, from Head of Human Resources to manager of a major change project, from managing an international acquisition to developing a business continuity plan. There is a very long list.

The major downside is, of course, that you never know when the next assignment will arrive nor from which direction. This can lead to a degree of stress. Instead of enjoying the free time, one starts worrying about the next assignment.

Looking for that next assignment, of course, can be almost a full time occupation in itself but it is important that one makes best use of the time off. A systematic approach to notifying contacts of availability, networking, updating of CV are all activities that fill the time between assignments. However, these tasks do not completely fill the time – it is essential that the Interim Manager has a range of other interests, work or social, that fill the time.

Without a doubt, Interim Management is my chosen career and I would not return to full time employment. There have been offers but after serious consideration they have been rejected.

4. Favourite assignment

Two are of particular interest. In 2000 I became involved with Balfour Beatty in the acquisition of a German-based rail engineering business. This particular assignment involved human resources due diligence in a company of about 1,500 employees based in eight countries. The challenges were to understand fully all areas of employment law (including TUPE and equivalent), and Company practice and to develop a full understanding of legal and other frameworks in each country. The preparation and presentation of a detailed due diligence report contributed to the decision to proceed with the acquisition.

The business was acquired and the focus switched to integration. The main emphasis was the establishment of new contracts and reward frameworks for senior managers and the establishment of shared service agreements for outsourced HR support in each country.

The end result of the assignment was that I had contributed to the acquisition and integration of a business into Balfour Beatty, which now is a significant part of its global success. Further acquisitions were made in subsequent years that complemented this growing sector of the company's business.

For me, one of the biggest rewards was being invited back to carry out further assignments, on two occasions.

One other assignment is of particular interest. This was was as Human Resources Director of a bank providing services mainly to the SME market. The Human Resources function had been severely criticised in an internal audit report, and required rebuilding. The HR Director was about to leave.

A complication was that a key member of the department was on long term sick leave, so with a team comprised almost entirely of Interims, turnaround was achieved and the requirements of the internal auditor met.

At the same time as this was happening, the bank was embarking on a merger with another part of the same group of companies, an investment bank. I was given the challenging role of managing the total merger process and heading the integration team. The creation of the new bank was achieved on time and within the established budget.

5. Conclusion

Interim Management is not for everyone. Finding the next assignment is the biggest challenge; one must develop the network to achieve this. There will be many disappointments – many prospective assignments come to nothing. Interim Providers are not always punctilious about keeping candidates informed nor do clients always make rapid decisions. This constant uncertainty and a certain amount of 'down-time' necessitate other interests to keep one busy and a degree of mental resilience that not all have.

But, for those who can constantly sell themselves, and have something to sell, *Interim Management provides the ultimate way of working.*

Chris Johnston

1. Life history

I started my professional career as a graduate trainee with a major insurance company but, after two rather dull and unfulfilling years, I moved into a human resource role with a packaging manufacturing subsidiary of British American Tobacco. I had been interested in the personnel field since university and the newly emerging employment legislation in the seventies meant that my law degree was a particularly useful entrée. I progressed up the management ladder within the same group of companies and was very fortunate that it was a successful organisation which doubled in size whilst I was there and so there were a lot of opportunities to gain experience in all areas of the profession, particularly in employee relations, since the company was a big player in the Printing industry at a time of major change and union unrest.

I wanted to broaden my commercial skills so I joined a smaller, privately owned, manufacturing company in the late 80s, as Personnel Director, because a management buyout was imminent. I had the rare opportunity to be part of a management team which doubled turnover and trebled profits before selling the business six years later. At the point where the business was sold it was time to move on and I seriously contemplated Interim work then but I felt that my professional skills would benefit from a spell back with a big organisation.

My next role was with a joint venture company set up by LucasVarity and Sumitomo of Japan. It was a challenging time for the JV because, as a first tier supplier to automotive OEM's, prices were being driven down so much that the transfer of the majority of the business to low cost central European countries was essential for survival – and it had to be finalised in two years, with no disruption to the supply of the safety-critical product. A new factory was established in Poland, quickly followed by another in Slovakia. The HR function was stretched to the limit because, as well as recruiting and training two entirely new workforces, totalling 2,500 people, to rigorous automotive standards, facilities in the UK had to be closed with a similar number of redundancies spread across three locations. The complexity of the task was enormous, particularly from a human resource perspective. We had some tough union battles. It was also critical to the plan that we persuade many of those who were to lose their jobs to train the new recruits and this meant moving large numbers of UK expatriates into central Europe. An added challenge was that it was necessary for Poles and Slovaks to spend time in the UK, living in the very communities where so many jobs were to be lost.

With the takeover of LucasVarity by TRW, I moved to a group role and there followed a roller-coaster two year period with merger activity focused on restructuring to maximise the benefit of the acquisition. I was responsible for a number of large, complex programmes, including downsizing and divestment; SAP implementation; and the introduction of Six Sigma; all of which fuelled my interest in project-based Interim work. During a lull, before embarking on another round of 'more of the same' restructuring tasks, I decided that the time was right to make the break and move into Consultancy/Interim.

2. Why IM?

Over the period I contemplated becoming a career Interim I saw the single biggest attraction as the potential for variety in the assignments. I enjoy short term projects, particularly those which are challenging and push the boundaries of my knowledge and capability. I have a low boredom threshold and can become rather frustrated when work becomes routine.

Most people of my generation have spent large amounts of time in only one organisation because loyalty was prized and service rewarded. Whilst I didn't fit that mould exactly, I certainly hadn't 'job-hopped' and, looking back, I can see that my work experience, whilst deep in many respects, lacked breadth in others. I looked on Interim work as a means to redress the balance, giving me the opportunity to experience different sectors, different locations and add a range of new professional strings to my bow.

The other aspects of the life didn't really weigh too prominently in my thoughts until I had been doing the work for a while. At the outset I considered them to be a bonus rather than the main reason for giving up my corporate life. I have never been enamoured with corporate politics, but it wasn't a reason for escaping and my work/life balance was poor but I was too macho to admit, even to myself, that it was sufficient reason to give up the relative security of highly paid regular employment.

I did a lot of research, before finalising my plan, and I satisfied myself that there was an adequate market for my skills. I dusted off parts of my network that had been neglected for years and registered with every Interim Provider I could find – the internet is a real winner for this. In the end, I was very fortunate in that a former boss offered me an excellent assignment to start as soon as I was available. I only had time to finalise my limited company status and arrange my professional indemnity insurance and I was then in the thick of a project to establish a new telecoms business in Brazil. The project went well and I even got paid in line with my newly developed business terms! I left at the end of the project, although I could have stayed to work on other, more routine, things. I decided that I was going to stick to my plan of only doing projects which really interested me. In the event, the expected new projects with new clients were a while coming and, whilst I had a great extended summer break with my family, I did start to get anxious about sourcing new work. With hindsight, perhaps I should have taken the opportunity to stay with my first client a little longer, but this must be a difficult call even for the most experienced Interims.

3. Likes and dislikes

The variety of projects was the main reason for becoming an Interim and that is still a real driver but, having experienced the life for approaching three years, other benefits have risen in prominence as I have adjusted to how things work.

My likes and dislikes are really the same issues from a different perspective. For example, I sometimes struggle with the uncertainties associated with winning the next project but I enjoy the quality time I have with my family during the gaps between assignments. I dislike the marketing process necessary to gain new assignments but I like meeting new people . . . and talking about myself. I savour the winning of a new assignment but I hate turning work away because a number of leads have come together at the same time.

I have really enjoyed the learning experiences – who says you can't teach an old dog new tricks? I've even enjoyed the processes involved in running my own limited company. I am one of those perverse people who enjoy dealing with the admin, accounts and VAT!

Meeting new people and learning about new businesses and environments, often in new locations remains a major plus for me. There is nothing quite like the buzz of walking into a new company and being confronted by a sea of new faces, not all friendly, and problems which need solving yesterday. Cost conscious businesses don't yet think of Interims as a first choice answer and *they don't usually bring Interims into steady-state situations.* A resource issue may have been festering for some time before a decision is reached, often because the decision makers were hoping that they might come up with an internal solution which they perceive to be cheaper. As a consequence there are invariably fires to fight and you really do have to hit the ground running but, in this sort of situation, there is usually a choice of areas where it is possible to make a quick impact which hopefully gives the client confidence in their decision to use an Interim Manager. Learning, afterwards, that you have influenced them to use Interims more readily in the future is another positive.

My biggest dislike remains the process of winning new assignments because the market is far from mature. I use my own network as far as possible but I keep in touch with the established Interim Service Providers. I have found their level of professionalism to be generally lacking, particularly in communication; I have often never even had the courtesy of an acknowledgement to an enquiry or, worse, no feedback once details have been presented to a client.

4. Favourite assignment

I honestly don't have one assignment that I have preferred over others. I have been lucky so far and I have enjoyed every assignment I have had, for differing reasons, though almost exclusively connected with the many and varied people with whom I have worked. A significant part of most of my projects to date has been to coach and mentor existing employees to enable them to perform better and I regard it as a personal achievement that so many of them keep in touch after an assignment has ended.

5. Conclusion

I made the right choice moving into the Interim world. It suits me both personally and professionally. I wish the market were better informed and more established so that it wouldn't be so difficult to get good assignments but I can see signs of improvement, even in the short time that I have been an interested party.

I have certainly achieved my objective of gaining variety and broadening my experience, not just from the HR perspective but also from running my own business.

Perhaps the best, and the most unexpected, thing has been that, by accident rather than design, my work-life balance is nearer where it ought to be and this has made a bigger difference to my life than I could ever have anticipated.

Neil Pirie

1. Life history

Educated at boarding school in Bedford, while his parents lived overseas (Royal Air Force), Neil excelled in everything non-academic; particularly things involving leadership and sport. He was Head of House, won the steeplechase two years running and was Captain of many sports.

At 18 Neil left school and completed a leading UK retailer's two year management training programme, which taught him the very basics. These basics have held true to Neil to this day and he often reflects on how good a foundation this was for his career.

At 20 Neil joined The Thomas Cook Group in their overseas sales and marketing department. Almost 25 years later Neil had visited over 150 countries in business, lived in Bahrain for 2 years, and Hong Kong twice – for 4 years each time. He travelled into Libya frequently, made 200 business trips to China and learnt some Arabic, Swahili, Cantonese and Mandarin – as well as a few words of Korean and Japanese.

His final post at Thomas Cook was Commercial Director, Financial Services and Group Director, India. He worked in both travel and financial services in a wide range of roles; and was a board director of many European boards for over 10 years. One of his final projects was a ground-breaking and radical re-structure of their Global Travellers Cheque business, which improved worldwide profitability by more than £34 million in a little over two years. He and his team wrote a book on their successes and failures.

He believes that a combination of a strict Scottish upbringing, his father being in the Royal Air Force and his being a boarder provided him with a very independent streak. His exposure to multicultural environments taught him more than a degree ever would have done, and provided him with practical hands-on experience. He believes very much in the 80/20 Pareto approach and regularly combines this with his significant intuition to ensure a decisive approach is taken, and once taken, implemented to the full.

He admits making many mistakes in his career and life, but at only 49, has been happily married for 28 years and has sons aged 25 and 22. Taking the risks of expatriate life three times he believes this has made him the leader he is today.

His biggest frustration with UK plc is that it's over-managed, under-led and too politically correct. He is not surprised that 90% of change programmes fail and believes there are two primary reasons: CEOs who protect their position and the status quo; and under-estimating the critical role communication plays.

Since 1999 Neil has been running his own Interim business.

2. Why IM?

When Neil left The Thomas Cook Group he had considerable time to review what he wanted to do with the remainder of his career. He was also recovering from a massive skiing accident. During this period he had access to considerable Outplacement, (very little of which he used). He reviewed carefully his corporate career looking for areas of similarity in the roles he had undertaken. He did not want to leave Peterborough, but realised that unless he commuted to London; his future had to be outside corporate life.

Against the advice of his outplacement counsellor, he opted to undertake the 'beginner's introduction to Interim Management', and remembers well meeting Nigel Corby for the first time in early 2000. He remembers thinking that of the 20 people on the programme with him, only one of two would actually cut it as interims and at that time he just hoped to be one of the two.

His decision was a conscious one and it was based on simple logic. Throughout his corporate career whenever there was a problem role, or problem managers or problem businesses he was always introduced to the challenge. When he had completed one, the next one came his way too. He remembers only having to attend a couple of specific internal interviews, as the jobs he got were lined up for him one after the other.

So his questions to himself were, could he:

1. Become self-employed and stay successful?
2. Maintain a decent standard of living?
3. Avoid having to move house from Peterborough?
4. Pay off his mortgage and pay for both of his sons' university fees?
5. Still enjoy a few more years at work?

He had never previously considered self employment, so had lots to learn. He used his network to avoid making too many beginners' mistakes and again holds up some of those conversations to this day as career enhancing. One of the classics he uses now when advising others considering self employment is not to skimp on the quality of business cards, stationery or a decent company name/logo. He spends much time coaching and counselling others considering self employment, only because he got so much help from others at a crucial time in his career/life.

3. Likes and dislikes

Likes include the freedom, the independence, the personal risks and the job satisfaction. As well as turning down offers of corporate employment. He enjoys being able to take long breaks between assignments. He enjoys the 'interview/business meeting' with prospective clients as he feels he is as much assessing their commitment as they are checking his out credentials. So much more "equal" than the corporate interview. He enjoys the success or failure of his personal toils, and knows that he can only blame himself for anything and everything. He enjoys golf in the summer and the respect that clients pay him. He enjoys not having to be political and toeing the company line when it's inappropriate for the business. He likes the lessons that the past 5 years have taught him, as well as the understanding he is able to pick up by working in a variety of different companies with different CEOs. He likes working only for CEOs, and would not consider a major change programme working for anyone except the CEO.

He dislikes the process of finding assignments – although to date every one of his assignments have been self-found, with no intermediary involvement. He dislikes having to pay so much of his company's earnings to the government and believes the 'system' under-rewards the self employed and over-rewards those in soft corporate roles. He cites as examples paid holidays, paid sickness, pension provision, and company car provision.

Overall he is far more pro than con – as the above clearly shows.

4. Favourite assignment

Neil was recruited by Clive Jacobs, founder and CEO of Holiday Autos. His initial position was that of Change Programme Director. This was into a truly entrepreneurial environment, where the CEO had a very hands-on approach.

He liked:

1. Clive's responsiveness to knowing the company needed to change
2. The freedom and trust Clive provided
3. The diversity of the role – 3 months after the assignment started Holiday Autos was acquired by Lastminute.com
4. Adapting to the needs of Lastminute.com
5. The permanent challenge of working on a .com

Although unable to provide specific figures yet on the outcome of Neil's assignment due to Lastminute.com being a quoted company, Neil more than surpassed the goals/objectives he was set in a forever changeable environment. The legacy he left was mostly in the people he supported and coached, as well as those who subsequently left the business. They remember his touches, his interventions, his apparently over-disciplinarian approach. He enjoyed working as member of the senior team without being an employee of the company. He enjoyed (very much) working with the very talented Clive Jacobs, Martha Lane Fox and Brent Hoberman. The investment in Neil unquestionably benefited many, and they know who they are.

5. Conclusion

Would Neil change the past 5 years of his career?

No way.

Why is that?

Well, let's review what he has achieved.

1. A move from a senior (cosseted) role in corporate life to self employment.
2. An understanding of NI, VAT, dividends and accountants.
3. Working in a range of different clients for a range of CEOs.
4. An average return on investment in him of over 50 times.
5. Delivering great value for money.
6. Delivering 'what it says on the tin' and more.
7. Learning from CEOs – both good and bad.
8. Coaching and supporting others – both clients and colleagues.
9. Even higher job satisfaction than before (and it used to be great).
10. Better quality of life.
11. More time with family.
12. Improved golf handicap.
13. What is earned is purely down to me and me alone.

Would he go back to corporate life again?

An interesting question. For the first 3 years Neil felt he had something to prove and he was absolutely focussed and determined to deliver, which he has done with some considerable success. However, now he has proved he can do it and "been there and done that" he will continue to review carefully all options.

Is he likely to still be a practising and professional interim in 5 years time?

Highly likely to be.

Stephen Jones

1. Life history

Deciding on a choice of career is never easy. Nevertheless, after graduating in Business Studies in 1973, I held the clear objective to win my first role which would use my skills to the full, offer a constant challenge to deliver value to my employer and provide opportunities for personal and professional advancement. I joined EMI in the international marketing department of one of their consumer products companies and have moved into international management roles of increasing responsibility ever since.

Development of business overseas for EMI led to a more senior role with Wolf Electric Tools, a privately owned power-tool company with great potential for overseas expansion. Management of exports to the Middle East and Africa led to appointment as General Manager of the Wolf distributors in Lagos, Nigeria, my first overseas posting. An interesting challenge, growing the business in an extremely difficult operating environment.

On returning from Nigeria I changed industry and joined the pharmaceutical company Wellcome as Regional Manager for Zaire. The remit was straightforward to describe but tough to implement. The goal was to re-establish Wellcome in Zaire in all product lines (ethical pharmaceuticals, consumer healthcare, insecticides and veterinary products). This to be achieved with pace to gain first-mover advantage over competitors who were also planning to re-enter the market. After setting up the local office, appointing appropriate sales and marketing staff and building distribution channels, my remit broadened to include management of the Wellcome business across Francophone Africa.

In 1986 I moved to Johnson and Johnson, to manage the consumer products business within the Europe, Middle East and Africa region. In addition to managing the development of business across 35 countries, responsibilities included development of third-party manufacturing in Iraq, Syria, Tunisia, Sudan, Zaire and Malta. Success and double-digit annual growth in revenue and profit over 5 years enabled major restructuring and strategic change to be successfully implemented.

In 1992 to broaden my business experience I moved from industry to consultancy, working in the healthcare and pharmaceutical practices of OASiS Group (now absorbed into the software company Sybase Inc) and from 1995 for two years with the global life sciences group at Cap Gemini.

After almost twenty years in industry and seven years developing consultancy business I decided to bring my accumulated experience to a different set of challenges. In 1998 I embarked on the next phase of my career, Interim Management.

2. Why IM?

After many years in industry in permanent roles why would I choose to change tack and become an Interim Manager? The answer is simple. Variety, challenge, excitement and flexibility. Let me explain.

However senior and exciting a 'permanent' role actually is, a significant element of the work this year will be the same as last year and likely will also be the same next year. Stop and analyse your own work for a few minutes. Does your analysis bear this out? You may well be managing by and large the same people you managed last year, the products may have changed slightly in some cases or there will have been launches of significant new products, the customers may broadly be the same and the challenges you face day to day will broadly be similar. None of this is true with Interim Management. A move to another Interim assignment will certainly expose you to a different management team and different peers and subordinates. It is likely to be a different culture and different business challenges too.

Against this changing background can be added two other important plusses: challenge and excitement. *Pace*, and by that I mean the speed at which you have to add value to the employer's business when you are working in an Interim Management role, drives the challenge and creates the excitement. This is not for the faint-hearted but for those who thrive in fast-moving environments. The need to deliver results quickly almost always adds to the excitement and challenge of working as an Interim. Why is there a need for speed? Simply put, the underlying cause is the perception held by some employers that Interim Managers are expensive. We all know they are not, but it remains a fact of Interim life that if business benefits are delivered fast, then the employer's perceptions of value for money will be much more favourable. It is no exaggeration when I say that it is quite usual to be asked to describe on the first Friday the achievements over the first five days. There is no honeymoon induction period! The Interim takes on board the brief prior to commencing the assignment and begins to validate the operating realities on the first day.

I mentioned flexibility as an important benefit to the Interim Manager. The traditional working model of, say, five weeks' holiday over the year combined with long hours does very little for the so-called work/life balance. Some do not mind putting work above all else but for those who do, then taking advantage of the usual gaps between assignments enables Interim Managers to spend time on the things they would not have time to do if they were in permanent employment. Unless an Interim is very lucky, assignments are rarely back to back.

To some extent the Interim Manager is the master of his or her destiny. Self-marketing in my experience can find new assignments provided this activity has focus. Networking is key. This flexibility is an important benefit from working as an Interim.

In addition to time, there are the financial implications of working as an Interim to take into account. It can be very rewarding providing assignments come up regularly. This is not always the case. Also one must consider that there are no fringe benefits like paid holidays, pension schemes, cars and the other trappings of permanent work. This is reflected in the daily rate which, when annualised, is almost always higher than the salary that an equivalent permanent role would command. This extra money should be carefully managed however. It is prudent to budget for the period of time when the assignments dry up and cash reserves are required to meet ongoing financial commitments.

3. Favourite assignment

Since 1998 I have been fortunate to complete seven assignments. These have ranged in duration from one month to 2 years. Clients included Advanced Medical Solutions plc an SME specialising in manufacture of advanced wound care products, Wyeth Inc the American healthcare giant and Procter & Gamble.

It is hard to select a favourite assignment because they have all been immensely challenging. However if I have to choose just one it would be the Clairol Division of Procter & Gamble for its scope, complexity and geographic reach. The Clairol assignment took the form of project with clearly defined scope and deliverables.

I was appointed Associate Director of European Customer Management, in February 2001, replacing the previous incumbent who had moved to McKinsey. Clairol was at that time owned by Bristol Myers Squibb who wished to divest their hair and skin care business, including Clairol, to provide cash for their core healthcare businesses. The uncertainty created by the divestiture made it impossible to recruit a permanent replacement. An Interim was the obvious solution.

The European Customer Management Project was 20% completed when I joined the company. Clairol, like many fast-moving consumer goods companies, had different trade prices for the same products in different countries across Europe. This in itself would not be a problem. However a significant proportion of Clairol's business was with multinational retailers like Carrefour, Ahold and Tesco who have operations across many countries. These price differentials were becoming more transparent as their IT infrastructure picked up the differences and made them visible to management. These differences *were* justifiable, but it became critical to build up a 'price defensibility rationale' to protect the business. If a major retailer successfully challenged the pricing and demanded that all prices be lowered to the lowest level being offered across Europe then revenues and profit would be significantly eroded!

The European Customer Management project required continuous collaboration of 18 key account managers located across Europe. Their reporting was within a matrix structure to their own country management, and to me for their input to the project over its duration. I also had four direct reports in the UK with responsibility for pricing and administration. The project focused on management of pricing to Clairol's top 7 European customers whose combined annual purchases were in excess of 30 million Euros. In addition, the Euro was being introduced across Europe during the lifetime of the project. This required decisions to be taken about psychological price points and conversion rates.

What were the key deliverables?

1. The Pricing Defensibility document running to 84 pages of data and factors justifying differences in pricing was produced and circulated to all key account managers across Europe. This enabled them effectively to justify pricing levels when challenged by customer management.
2. An IT system was built, tested and rolled out across Europe to enable all trade terms and pricing information to be updated in real time at country level. This system enabled 'pricing risk' to be calculated at any point in time to underpin strategic pricing decisions by the Board.
3. A pricing decision process was designed and adopted by the Pricing Review Board (Associate Director European Customer Management and other senior Management Committee members). This process enabled all pricing risks to be fully evaluated before new products were launched or price changes were applied to current products
4. Pricing 'corridors' were developed. Trade prices for each product would be adjusted over an agreed period so that they fell within the pricing 'corridors'. These had a variance of 15% between the lowest and highest prices.
5. Overall pricing risk across Europe was reduced by more than 1.6 million Euros in a full year. This meant that even if the Top 7

customers successfully challenged price differentials, the reduction
in profit would be 1.6 million Euros less than it would have been
if the project had not taken place

This strategic project could not have been completed without the
complete cooperation and input from an excellent team across Europe
and my UK direct reports. The European team had their own
day-to-day sales responsibilities and all employees were also facing the
possibility that they may not have a role when the business transferred
into new ownership.

Transition of the team through the divestiture process was also part
of my responsibilities. Maintenance of morale and commitment
required strong leadership skills. Only two staff chose to leave during
the 13 month duration of the project.

In addition to managing the project, I ensured that my UK staff
were fully considered for roles in the company when ownership
transferred.

This project was completed on time and within budget. When
Procter & Gamble completed their purchase of Clairol in the first
quarter of 2002 they were able to assimilate easily the European
business with the Top 7 customers.

4. Conclusion

Interim Management is not for everyone. It can be lonely and
dauntingly challenging. It requires courage, high energy, credibility and
the ability to add value quickly. It is not for the faint-hearted. But for
those who choose Interim Management as a career option the personal
rewards can be high

Simon Marks

1. Life history

My first job after graduating from Reading University with a BSc. in
Agricultural Economics in 1977 was as a production buyer with Ford
Motor Company in Essex. I left there six years later and joined Valor
Heating in Birmingham as Purchasing Manager. Cast adrift from the
warm support cocoon of a global corporate I joined the Chartered
Institute of Purchasing & Supply, and soon realised that full
membership would, in time, be the essential qualification for any job
in this function. After three years of night school I passed my final
exams. Sure enough the next job I applied for demanded CIPS

membership, and armed with my new qualification I moved on after five years and joined Kalamazoo.

That job lasted four years ending in redundancy as a result of a business reorganisation during which I worked myself out of a job. That said, Kalamazoo was the most interesting 'permanent' job I had, acting as a 'fixer' for the Finance Director for the last two years, managing amongst other things the sales ledger and car fleet. After a few months of job search I found what turned out to be my final permanent job with Glynwed as Facilities Manager based primarily on my car fleet management experience. It too ended in redundancy; after three years.

I started the job search over again with the assistance of an Outplacement consultant provided by the company, and using my records from three years earlier. It seemed that potential employers to whom I applied for procurement jobs saw my having been out of main stream buying as a barrier. While looking for a 'career enhancing opportunity' I took two jobs as a contract Purchasing Manager to re-establish my credentials and put bread on the table. I found that I thoroughly enjoyed the challenge, and I got a buzz knowing that I was really needed rather than filling a position in an organisation chart whether there was a full time job to be done or not.

At 40 years of age I realised that my first job lasted six years, the next five, then four and the last just over three years; and my boredom threshold was getting lower. Even if the next job was to be for five years I would then be 45, and the job after that may well be my last. In 1995 there was no legislation under consideration to outlaw age discrimination as there is now, and the prevailing view was that at 50 you were too old. With my record could I really anticipate being with the same company for twenty years?

One of the contract jobs was through a network contact who worked with a consultancy that amongst other things operated in the Interim Management marketplace, and although they placed me as a sole trader, it got me thinking about the options. I had applied for many attractive permanent roles and although I was invited to interview on a number of occasions no job offers resulted. Was I, as far as permanent employment was concerned, over the hill at 40?

2. Becoming an interim

The satisfaction I got from the second temporary contract made my decision for me. I would no longer invest massive amounts of emotional capital with each job application form sent off, suffer sleepless nights before interview, plan for possible relocation and cope with the disappointment of rejection. I stopped applying for permanent jobs and began registering with Interim Intermediaries using the ATIES booklet as a starting point and I wrote a business plan as the first steps towards establishing my personal services company.

One permanent job that I had applied for was as Supplies Manager for a company in aerospace, but the agency told me I was rejected because although I met all their other criteria I did not have any aerospace experience. My argument that there was a department of 27 to manage who did have the specific industry experience, and I would in any case rely on their knowledge for the detail did not appear to win the day. In late November 1996, shortly after the second contract finished, out of the blue, the recruitment agent called. 'Was I working?' Their client Dunlop Aviation were going live with a SAP3 implementation over the New Year shut down and would I go for an interview as an Interim as they had been unable to recruit someone to fill the job. '*Only* as an Interim Manager because now I would not consider the job as a permanent employee" was my reply. The week I started was also the week registration of my 'Nomis Associates Ltd.' came through. By January Dunlop Aviation decided that lack of aerospace experience was not after all a deal breaker and they offered me the job. Too late. I had made my decision to make Interim a career and was not about to fall at the first hurdle. The emotional, intellectual and physiological commitment had been made, with the support of my wife, and there was no going back.

That assignment lasted only four months, but within six weeks I was working again, this time living in the Forest of Dean. That job lasted until Christmas, followed by what turned out to be a twelve months job close to my home in Birmingham, starting in January 1998. I was hooked on the excitement that comes with change, and the challenges presented by new places, businesses and people, all to be learned in double quick time.

After two good years I hit a tough patch. Between January 1999 and March 2000 I had one job lasting from April to September. Six months work in fifteen months! Financially this was not a complete disaster as my wife and I agreed, when I wrote the business plan, to live on a budget and from the beginning we paid ourselves the same quarterly amount by way of salary and dividend, irrespective of whether or not I was invoicing. But there was no bonus for two years.

The worst part of not working is that you self-confidence takes a hit. You start to wonder.

'*Will I get another job at the same or better day rate than last time?*'

'Should I have accepted that job offered to me at a lower rate than normal rather than holding out to at least match my rate from last time?'

Or worse still *'Should I consider that permanent job I just know could be mine for the asking?'*

The positive feelings that flow from being on assignment contrast sharply with the feelings you experience when not working. When working you have a very busy week, earning good money, with the sense of being valued (despite your cost), and being part of a team with a real job to do. Weekends are spent catching up on running your Limited Company and other regular chores.

When you have been at home for three or four months and your partner suggests forcibly that you should be out at work, things can get difficult. There is a limit to the networking, marketing and admin you can find to do. I have established a routine that includes always getting up early and never watching daytime TV. It limits the downside, but you still aren't part of a team, and you're still not invoicing. But the change and contrast is all part of the thrill of being an Interim, if you can stand it.

One other big challenge is holidays. When do you take them? When the assignment finishes? But then you might miss out on a super job while you are away. When you are working? And take the double whammy of lost income and the cost of the holiday? There is no right answer, but if you don't take a holiday some time – and the period between assignments is certainly not a holiday – just what are you working for?

3. Favourite assignment

My favourite assignment was also the toughest, and maybe that was part of it. The client was an Aerospace company in Surrey where the Purchasing Manager had been off on secondment for some nine months. Things came to a head when a Baan implementation, an IiP audit and a factory move all became imminent, and the Purchasing Department was failing in its core responsibility to support production. The contractor who had been trying to hold things together stepped aside, but he stayed on to support me working along side the Senior Buyer.

Without a manager to champion the department, every production problem had been blamed on the buyers, and morale had slumped. I reorganised the buyers into commodity teams to support each other and developed Key Performance Indicators. We investigated every supply failure, and that normally showed the root cause lay upstream of purchasing. This led to the commissioning of complete review of the supply chain from order intake through build scheduling to production, to identify the fundamental weaknesses in the business that had previously been masked as poor purchasing performance.

With HR, I rewrote all the job specifications and introduced salary scales to emphasis the importance of purchasing professionalism, and by the time I left three buyers had signed up to follow the CIPS course of study. The manager who had been away on secondment left the business, and we recruited a CIPS qualified replacement who was still in post three years later. All the initial objectives were met, and Purchasing had been transformed from an order-processing function into a professional department that could play a full role in the business.

4. Conclusion

I have been an Interim Manager since 1996 and would never consider a 'proper job' again. I now have complete confidence that I will win another assignment at the right rate and am able to enjoy the 'resting periods'. When looking for work after an assignment finishes, it is through a network of intermediaries, contacts, colleagues and friends. I never have to explain why I 'lost my job' because all assignments come to a conclusion, which is not a failure to be explained, but an opportunity to take up a new challenge.

Tony Hurley

1. Life history

A childhood following an Army father around the world eventually saw me settle as an adolescent in Barrow-in-Furness on the Cumbrian coast. There I finished my schooling and an apprenticeship followed with the town's biggest employer, Vickers Limited. Here 14,000 people were employed in shipbuilding and engineering.

This period with Vickers was an exciting time with new technology, international travel and further education leading to a good honours degree. In my mid 20s I was given an extraordinary promotion to lead a project to finalise the design and introduce into production a new product, which to that point had failed as a programme on technical requirement, timescale and cost. With 25 engineers and draughtsmen it was an intense period successfully concluded. The result of this was I was sponsored and gained a Fellowship in Manufacturing Management at Cranfield University. This was an 18-month programme to attract qualified engineers into production. For me it was a turning point as after some 14 years in the Defence industry it opened my eyes to commercial business and more importantly gave me greater self-confidence in my abilities.

Following the Fellowship, Vickers had been nationalised by the Government and I left to join the real world. I worked for a number of companies in the industrial North of England. In all cases I was heavily involved in initiating change in difficult industrial relations environments. I learnt more from seeing things done badly than done well. After operating at production and plant level I took up my first Managing Director position at 38 years old. This was a turn-around situation and my first responsibility for the whole of a business. The company became financially stable and had a good medium-term position even in a declining market. After five years I moved to do two more major changes to businesses before joining a leading company in the electrical engineering field.

This engineering company had grown through acquisition and I had, in my sector, two sites, duplicating work. As well as day-to-day business, a plan was to be developed to create one new facility. This initial planning was to be done with no reference to other personnel due to its sensitivity. I was able to assess the market, visit competitors and equipment manufacturers and eventually design, cost and plan the implementation of this new facility. Once the changes were declared the programme was implemented following a good deal of discussion and negotiation with trade unions and individuals. The end result was the implementation of a £3 million investment on time and to budget, a very busy year. This facility employed some 200 people and had the capability to be the UK leader in its field.

2. Why Interim Management?

Once this new facility and its support team had been put into place I was surprised then on the involvement (=interference?) from so many people who had kept away when the turmoil was happening. This was compounded with a change in the Group sales focus, which tried to grow market share in the Middle East where the competition was low-cost Eastern Europe and Far East manufacturers. Perhaps I had become too close to the project and how I felt it should be developed but the result was that I decided to leave. I put my notice in and then set about finding a new role. My leaving was kept quiet and indeed I worked a further seven months before my leaving was announced.

During this period I started the usual trawl of the permanent job market and this had its ups and downs.

I do not know what exactly made me say, 'I will become an Interim'. I had employed an Interim cost accountant myself in the recent past; I was interviewed by an Interim on my job search – as a permanent replacement for him. It was probably this growing awareness of the industry and my own reassessment of my career that said *I wish to be more in control of my life.* After years of turning around businesses and realising that I was motivated by successfully introducing change, I was lead quickly to the conclusion that I would be suited for this career. So in preparation I built up my marketing plan, laid out a monthly 3-year budget (corporate habits die hard) and attended the introduction seminar organised by the Interim Management Association. Perhaps more importantly we had been able to build up a financial buffer, which gave both my wife and me that bit of confidence about the start up. I will admit to being quite surprised as to how well my partner took to the idea of this way of life.

So we had seven months phasing out of a permanent position, building up the marketing pack and starting the network of contacts.

Within a month of being on my own I received a call from a contact at a university. A company that had a vital new product that was a year late to market and was already being matched by the competition. Contact was made with the General Manager and a factory visit led to discussions on the definition of the project, rates and conditions, particularly payment terms. Within the week I started my first assignment as a Project Manager. This lead to handling a further project and the development of a training programme for the teams on the concept of project management.

This first assignment brought home to me a number of key aspects of the Interim role. Firstly you need to be hands on and often carry out duties that will have been well below the status level you have held before. Secondly you see so many things going wrong in the company well outside your brief that it is dangerous to stray too far into them. Finally even though you are there on a temporary basis you cannot avoid the politics! Even if you know you are going to leave them behind they can negatively effect your assignment. By the way both new product programmes were recovered.

3. Likes and dislikes

After five years and nine assignments, Interim Management still gives me the satisfaction I need in my life and career. The constant change in company, different markets and different personalities to deal with all make for enjoyment as well as frustration. It is fascinating how different markets have similar problems and challenges yet every one believes they are unique. I have been pleasantly surprised how quickly I have been able to assimilate to new roles and this is no doubt due to the broad experiences I gained before becoming an Interim.

On each assignment I have also learnt new skills particularly computer skills. Up to working as an Interim I have never needed to use e-mail or personally handle many software packages. Now people look to me to show them. Constantly I see the demand made for me to mentor people within the client company, sometimes informally, sometimes formally. The advantage of being independent and transient helps often in allowing people to feel at ease with such support.

The loneliness, as an Interim, due to lack of the support systems and social aspects that you would find in a permanent position, was another challenge to meet. For the natural networker this may be easy to overcome but does need hard work from others including myself. I have found that investing in formal training has helped particularly in newer themes and technologies. This builds up the confidence not only in being able to talk the language of new philosophies but also to realise that many are just extensions to more fundamental skills one has developed over the years. There is no doubt that to stay in the Interim business you need to be self-sufficient and set your professional development plans.

No matter in what context you are introduced to a company there are always the politicians who can and often do make your life very difficult. It is easy to say that, as you know you are not staying with the business, you just put up with it and work around it. Such characters do not reserve their destructive tactics for Interims only though and I believe the Interim is a more objective observer than the client's senior managers. This just confirms a personal theory that the true added-value in a business is more positively affected by team working than by vocational skills.

The main advantage I saw in becoming an Interim was to be in control of my own life. This has, in reality, not been as clean cut as I had imagined though. The idea of finishing an assignment then saying 'I'll just have 3 months off then pick up the next job' is too optimistic. Like the proverbial bus, assignments do not appear just when you want them. Marketing then becomes a full time task and eats into free time. This also brings about a sense of insecurity, which both the Interim and the family need to be prepared for.

On three occasions I have been asked to join the client company as a permanent employee. This is obviously flattering but overall the independence argument will always win with me.

4. Favourite assignment

I took on an assignment with a Defence company. The Production Manager had been given a critical assignment himself and I was to fill his day-to-day role for some 3 months. Challenges had been set for productivity and the budget for that year. There were some 200 personnel in the operation, most of whom were skilled technicians.

There is no doubt that some industries operate at a faster pace than others and that their expectations vary. It soon became clear that, as we chased production output, failure was accepted. This was as long as an excuse could be given. So an early part of the culture change was to ensure that when a plan did not work, or looked as though it would fail for whatever reason, then a recovery plan was put into place. Persistence with this over a number of months was needed before the message stuck. There were some process improvement programmes already underway at this time. I was able to support these and enhance their benefits by the introduction of group working, improved operating cells for each product line and involving the groups directly with their customers.

In parallel with this there was a programme of absorbing the work from another site in the group. This meant the closure of that operation and the transfer of all facilities. Although similar, there were significant differences in skill sets and customer requirements. The programme was stuck at the starting blocks and no significant project planning had been carried out. A showdown meeting was soon to be held with the customer. I was nervous about it, let alone the customer whose product was affected. On my own initiative I produced detailed project plans, which were accepted just prior to the meeting by the client's senior director. The customer understood the plans and though they were not happy at this stage we could at least give the impression we had the programme under control.

From this point I assumed the project management of the co-location. I reorganised the management team. We then set about the recruitment of 100 extra technicians along with their training programmes, developed the production planning over the transfer period and organised the physical transfer of stocks and facilities.

The plant engineering was one aspect to which I could contribute directly. All the other requirements needed the detailed knowledge of the experienced management team. This is a key understanding for any Interim Manager. You have to rely on the client's team with their detailed skills, yet have the managerial experience to lead and direct such teams. I believe being a successful Interim makes you a better manager. You rely on people, not on your superior product knowledge.

This programme took over a year, cost £2.6 million, was to time and the customers' deliveries were seamless throughout. It was a great team effort.

In the meantime the day job was still carried out and confidence was built up with other customers. The facility is the finest of its type in Europe and still runs extremely well today. Its only threat is within the control of defence reviews.

I have had repeat business from this client since.

5. Conclusion

At this stage I see Interim Management as being what I will do for the rest of my career in industry. The independence, having some control over my own future and the variety all contribute to me enjoying this. Most importantly I am still learning and being an Interim makes me a better manager.

Noelle Bowden

1. Career background

Noelle Bowden entered the National Health Service on the National Training scheme in 1977 after graduating from The University of Sheffield with a degree in Business Studies. She trained in the North Western Region; gained her professional qualification from The Institute of Healthcare Managers and started her climb up the NHS managerial career ladder. After posts within the Manchester Teaching Hospitals, Noelle went to the Blackpool Victoria Hospital as Deputy General Manager. The Victoria is a large District General Hospital covering all general medical specialties. Whilst in Blackpool, Noelle got her Masters degree in Health Service Management from the University of Manchester. She then moved to St James Hospital ('Jimmies') in Leeds, as Director of Operations and later Director of General Services.

2. Why Interim Management?

In 1998, the two Teaching Hospitals in Leeds merged, and, as is the way with these things, Noelle's post was made redundant.

'When you are on the career ladder, you do not think of jumping off, but when you are pushed off, you start to think about different options' said Noelle.

So, at the time, Noelle did not start applying for permanent posts in the NHS, but she had a germ of an idea that the NHS has locum doctors and agency nurses – why not locum managers? Reading the ATIES Guide to Interim Management helped to crystallise Noelle's thoughts and with a determination that she was an Interim Manager not a management consultant, she incorporated her company as Noelle Bowden Management Ltd. in 1999.

Work was slow in coming. Noelle registered with all the major agencies and then began the dreaded cold (and warm) calling. She had a lot of contacts after over 22 years in the NHS, but it was difficult. Firstly explaining about her redundancy and then explaining the concept of Interim Management to a profession that had never encountered it. It was May 1999 before Noelle got her first assignment and in truth that assignment was a collection of small consultancy projects – but it was work!

Since then, the assignments have come steadily along. Noelle has managed:

Medicine in Dewsbury
Clinical Support Services in South Manchester
Surgery in Bedford; South Manchester and East Kent

She has also been the Assistant Chief Executive at Maidstone & Tunbridge Wells. As this article is written, she is about to start a new assignment as Director of Operations at Barking, Havering & Redbridge.

Noelle intersperses these major assignments with either consultancy/project work or holiday.

3. Likes and dislikes

'I enjoy the challenge of Interim Management' says Noelle. She relishes the steep learning curve at the start of an assignment, and takes pride in a thorough, detailed handover at the end. And in the middle? 'All of my assignments have yielded results' says Noelle. 'I specialise on improving performance – either general performance required for the Trust's national rating or financial performance.' Running her own business (albeit a small one) is also something Noelle enjoys.

When asked about her favourite assignment, Noelle admits she has enjoyed most of them and says it would not be fair to single out one.

Of course Interim Management does have its downsides. The search for the next assignment is always a task that one wishes to put off until the next day. Living away from home during the week is endured not enjoyed The support of a permanent peer group, and the provision of professional development are taken for granted in a permanent post but as an interim – if you don't develop yourself no one will do it for you!

Interim Management has enabled Noelle to combine her skills and experience as a hospital manager in a more diverse way than the traditional career path. She would not take a permanent post in the NHS (despite receiving offers!). Interim is not for everyone, but Noelle's germ of an idea that there was a niche in the market for interim NHS managers has been proven to be true and is providing a rewarding career for her.

III The Interim Management Association

The Interim Management Association (IMA), is the trade association of the Interim Management Service Providers and is a specialist sub-division of the Recruitment and Employment Confederation.

The Association was formed in 1987 as the 'Association of Temporary and Interim Executives Services', (ATIES) with the aim of allowing the companies operating in the fledgling industry to share information and to exchange ideas. The Association expanded rapidly in the 1990s and was re-branded and re-launched in 2000 to become the IMA.

Today the Association has 3 main aims:

1. To promote the Interim Management industry.
2. To set and monitor standards within the industry
3. To become recognised as the voice of the industry.

Promotion. The re-launch was significant for more than just the name change. It was brought about by the growing realisation that effective, collective action was needed to develop the industry which still had the appearance of being fragmented. The members accepted a significant rise in subscriptions to generate an effective budget for marketing and PR activities. This has continued and 2005 was important, as an 'Industry Champion' was appointed, primarily to raise the profile of the industry and to develop wider links with industry, commerce, other professional bodies and academia.

Standards. The Association sets high standards for entry and all members have to have been trading as a company or an independent and identifiable division for a minimum of 3 years, placing over 80% of their Interim Managers in assignments in excess of around £500 a day. In addition they must confirm annually that they abide by the IMA Code of Practice and accept the Association's disciplinary procedures. As a consequence the membership is still less than 10% of the companies claiming to work in the interim market place but their collective turnover is in the order of 80–90% of all assignments placed through third parties.

Representation. Finally the Interim Management Association aspires to become recognised as the voice of the Interim Management industry, representing its interests at governmental level both nationally and internationally.

Further information about the Interim Management Association and its members can be found on their website:

www.interimmanagement.uk.com

(IV) *The Institute of Interim Management*

The rapid growth of the interim market in the 1990s led to an overwhelming demand from professionals operating as interim mangers to have their own professional body to set:

1. Recognised and accredited quality standards for the professional Interim Manager.
2. A framework for ethical standards of behaviour, performance and continued professional development.

The establishment of the Institute of Interim Management, IIM, marked an important stage in the development of Interim Management as a recognised professional discipline. With the encouragement and support of the Interim Management Association and the Chartered Management Institute, (CMI), a meeting of Interim Managers was convened in Corby and a Steering Committee was set up. The IIM was formally launched in April 2001.

Until August 2002, the IIM operated as a 'special interest group' of the CMI. However given the IIM's growing need for greater emphasis on its own special area of management, and to facilitate a higher profile for Interim Management within industry and commerce, in August 2002 the IIM opted for independent status. Since September 2002 the IIM has been a fully independent professional institute incorporated as a not-for-profit organisation limited by guarantee.

From the outset the IIM has sought to establish professional standards for Interim Managers by implementing a strong accreditation process for membership, and placing great emphasis on Continuing Professional Development, (CPD). The IIM with its assessed standards for membership provides a welcome step forward for the industry.

The Vision for the IIM is:

... to be recognised as the pre-eminent body for quality standards of accreditation, professional development and best practice for practitioners of Interim Management in the UK, which will lead to the development of Interim Management both in the UK and internationally

In addition the IIM provides a network of contacts for its members, a series of regional events for members and potential members, an informative monthly newsletter and a range of membership services.

More information on the Institute of Interim Management can be found on their website at:

www.ioim.org.uk

(V) *Continuing Professional Development*

Most professions these days expect their members to undertake some form of Continuing Professional Development, CPD, and this is particularly important in Interim Management where one of the attractions for a potential client is access to modern , current management skills and expertise. CPD in its crudest form is merely a systematic means of recording the steps that an individual has taken to stay fully up to date but it does bring with it a number of other benefits:

- Improvement and enhancement of a professional status
- Staying abreast of current thinking, market changes and legislative developments
- Achieving higher standards of personal performance
- Ability to anticipate and instigate positive change more effectively

CPD is generally accepted as being a personal responsibility although most professional institutes give their members a framework, with associated documentation based on the generally accepted CPD cycle:

- Establish current development needs
- Set learning/development objectives
- Undertake development
- Check development against objectives
- Record the results
- Evaluate the benefits/shortcomings
- Address how this may be improved

The problem for the aspiring Interim Manager however is that you are likely already to belong to the body representing your core profession, for example the Chartered Management Institute, Chartered Institute of Marketing, Chartered Institute of Personnel and Development, Association of Chartered Accountants and so on. All of these require evidence of CPD to improve or even maintain professional status and requirement to show CPD as a practicing interim can be seen as an additional burden.

The Institute of Interim Management has the following advice to offer:

Is CPD optional?

The IIM believes that there is a professional obligation for all Interim managers to undertake CPD and to remain 'sensibly over-qualified' for their roles. As such, a statement of commitment to CPD is required on joining the Institute. Regular investment of time in learning should be seen as an essential part of life for a professional Interim manager. In your own interest, members are advised to treat CPD as a mandatory activity rather than an optional one.

What counts as CPD?

Development should begin from the member's own current knowledge base. Any activity or practice which helps a member to operate more effectively as an Interim manager should be a relevant part of his/her CPD program.

Keeping up-to-date with relevant literature, leadership activities in sport, voluntary, business arenas or attendance at other non-IIM events are also viewed as critical elements of a successful programme. There is no one prescribed way of applying the concept – members should evolve the method(s) they find to be the most beneficial.

How much CPD is required?

The appropriate amount of CPD will vary according to individual members' needs and circumstances. The minimum is that needed to maintain competence and stay up-to-date, however, simply meeting a minimum standard is not sufficient. The IIM believes that individual CPD programmes should be *continuous* and *focused*, with the aim of improving personal competence and performance.

What processes should be followed in recording and assessing CPD?

The IIM recommends a process where members create and maintain their own personal *CPD Development Plan* (which identifies their specific needs) and *CPD Development Log* (which records details of activities).

Further guidance and advice, specific to Interim Management, can be found on the IIM website at:

www.ioim.org.uk

 *Just CVs*

Get your CV right – and keep it right!

A CV is not, *definitely* not just a record of your life in business.

A CV is a piece of sales literature

It is your principal ambassador-at-large. It will be working all day and every day for you, in clients' and Interim Service Providers' data bases. So you have to make sure it SELLS for you. Review again Chapters 6 and 7. *Make sure you are really clear in your mind* about the difference between a *feature* (e.g. 'I was the Director of Manufacturing'), and a *benefit or achievement* (e.g. 'I improved productivity by 43% over three years'). *Clients buy your achievements and the benefits to them!*

We recommend your CV has the following outline structure:

1. Name, address, telephone
2. Profile – a summary statement of your Niche Position.
3. History of *Achievements* as an independent.
4. History of *Achievements* in employment.
5. Qualifications/personal

We are indebted to John Webster for the following 5 sample front pages. We have assumed that most of our examples are beginners at Interim Management, so do not have records of achievement yet as Interims:

MICHAEL JAMES

Ashwell Cottage, Great Bar, Cumbria, LA2 12 CT
Telephone: (Home) 01547 908080 (Mobile) 0555 26
(Business) 01547 616161

Interim Manager and Management Consultant, with Managing/Manufacturing/Quality Director background in SME's, (£10–£350 million) in light, medium and heavy Engineering, Scientific Instruments, Nuclear Submarine power transmission systems, Railway equipment, Foundries and Nuclear Power equipment.

Wide experience of Multi-site manufacturing management, including setting up and closing large and small sites. Direct control of unionised labour-forces, up to 20,000 people. Also experience of non-unionised teams of up to 200.

Board-level roles included Cunard Shipbuilding and Engineering, British Rail Engineering. Also Executive Committee member for Crosby Instruments; Divisional Council member and Chair of NW Railway Division of I. Mech. E. Trustee, Shipbuilding Industries Pension Fund.

- Restructured manufacturing operations, closing 5 plants and laying off 10,000 people across the UK. Manufacturing experience in Germany, Switzerland and Italy. Converted BR wagon repair works, (2,200 personnel), to carriage refurbishment works.
- Member of Crosby Instruments Executive Committee, turned loss of £38 million to £7 million profit in 2 years.
- Business development, sales and customer service experience in USA, Africa, Europe and Scandinavia. Managed contracts up to £400 million.
- Human Resources, mentoring and counselling experience at all levels, in organisations from 50 to 2,500 personnel. Able to transform people's attitudes, in the workplace and facing customers, producing bottom-line effects in the millions of pounds.
- 10 year's experience of liaison with Government, up to Minister levels.
- Significant CAPEX development and appraisal, ranging from departments to entire divisions, including extensive IT-based systems expenditure.

CAREER SUMMARY

CURRENT – Self-employed Consultant/Interim Manager

2002–05 Crosby Instruments – Personnel and Quality Director

1998–02 Cunard Shipbuilding and Engineering – Project Director, Total Quality.

1989–98 Cunard Shipbuilding and Engineering – Managing/ Manufacturing Director.

1969–89 British Rail Engineering – rising to Manufacturing Director.

Qualifications: CEng., FI Mech.E., MIEE., MIOM. Age 56

GEORGE ROBERTS Dip. MS MCIPS

Highland Meadow, Rivermead, York LE45 26LT
Telephone 01375 375 375

Interim Managing Director – experience of manufacture, assembly and sale of Construction/Building products for commercial, domestic and DIY use. Operations from £7–£75 million turnover, involving multiple warehousing, control of large vehicle fleets, servicing 100 retail outlets from 8 UK depots. Interim roles have included corporate disposal, site refurbishment/closure, redundancies and new product development. Strong reputation with suppliers, major merchant and construction groups, hospital trusts, airport authorities, and hotel/leisure sectors.

Troubleshooting successes:
- As Interim CEO for Derbyshire Quarries, devised and implemented a plan that generated £1.5 million extra cashflow, and transformed a disposal candidate into a strong profit performer in 6 months. Mentored inexperienced MD to improve performance and prospects.
- Increased sales at Reynolds Timber from £12 million to £17 million p.a. and devised new operational controls – turning £2 million loss into breakeven in 18 months.
- Devised and marketed new strategic service for Qualitas Bathrooms that produced £1 million extra sales in first year.
- As Operations Director of 7 factories for Plastitube, initiated sell-off of 75 vehicle fleet and contracted – out distribution, saving £1.5 million p.a. Negotiated revised contracts with gas, oil and coal suppliers, total saving £2 million p.a.
- Reduced Conway Glass's procurement costs by £750K p.a. Implemented revised operational controls that increased profits by a further £500K per annum.

CAREER BACKGROUND
20 + years' direct experience of the manufacture and sale of Building products, including: timber moulding and treatments, furniture components; laminating; sanitary ware; plumbing and corporate washrooms; industrial coatings; adhesives and waterproofing; bituminous and slate roofing; aerated concrete; stone building and civil engineering products.

CAREER SUMMARY

2001–05 Qualitas Bathrooms – General manager
1998–2001 Reynolds Timber – Operations Director and acting CEO
1997 Derbyshire Quarries – Acting CEO
1990–96 Cornwall Slate – Sales and Marketing Director
1985–1990 Plastitube – Operations Director, Divisional and General manager, from Materials Manager.
1980–85 Conway Glass – Materials Manager
1978–80 Roberts Construction, Senior Buyer
1970–78 National Coal Board, rising to Deputy Purchasing and Stores Manager
Age:54

CHRISTOPHER CHARLES BA Hons.

14 Main Street, Robover, Warwick, WR10 5QZ
Telephone: (HOME) 0122 779 933. (OFFICE) 0115 958 9583

Sales and Marketing Director of £80 million plc. Divisional Sales and Marketing Director in £150 million plc. 21 years' experience of frozen, chilled and packaged Grocery foods. Strong reputation with branded and private-label products with all major retail groups, including Tesco, Asda, Sainsbury, Iceland, Morrison, Somerfield etc. Advertising, TV campaign and PR skills, to £5 million budgets. European product launches, successful acquisitions.

KEY CAREER ACHIEVEMENTS

- In the past 5 years created and launched innovative new product range for Carters plc that added £50 million cumulative sales and pioneered the development of a new £80 million frozen food sector. Recruited NPD team and managed departmental team of 8 Account Managers.
- Launched product range into Italy. Formed strategic alliance with Dutch poultry supplier.
- Extensive margin management experience. Initiated improving GM for key business sector that added £3 million p.a. to profits. Reduced £3 million packaging costs by 10%.
- New brands conceived and launched:
  Carters' Vegetable grills and burgers.
  Rosemary's Marmalades/Hartlepool jams
  Birds' ready meals and pizzas.

Crestco own label prepared sliced meats.

Introduced Kollagos into the UK.

Pioneered prepared salads and dips market for Matthews.

Regional speciality sausages and pies for Meridian.

- Created new sales-forecasting, production and distribution scheduling, and promotional programme that reduced over-heads and stockholding by 10%, (£300K), and raised service levels from 80% to 97%.

EMPLOYMENT BACKGROUND.

1993–2005 Carters. – Sales Director , promoted to be Group Sales and Marketing Director

1991–93 Welshpool Foods – Marketing Manager

1985–91 Kennedy Frozen Meats – Product Group Manager

1981–85 Harris and Settle, Advertising Agency – Account manager

1978–81 Martins Chocolates – Salesman, Marketing Assistant.

Age 45

NORMA COLLINS BEng. Hons., CEng. MI Mech Eng.

1. Forest Meadows, Plymouth, PL37 6HH. Telephone: 01752 724883

Managing Director of 4 divisions of a £32 million electronics group. Progressive career from Development Engineer with Rolls Royce. Awards with Internal Electronics, (USA). 20 years' involvement in Aerospace, Naval Weapons Systems, Oil and Gas, Electronics, Power Generation, manufacturing and engineering. Companies from £2 million to £500 million. Wide corporate Troubleshooting experience, improving engineering and IT systems, reducing headcounts and other costs, creating better profit results. High success in product development and winning new business in USA, Europe and Japan.

KEY CAREER DETAILS

Specific PROFIT improvements:

- Turned £1 million p.a. loss into £1.2 million profit, and cash flow from – £700k to + £600k in 18 months.
- Reduced inventory by 50%, improving cash by £5 million. Improved MRP system, cutting order backlog by £2.5 million.
- Regularly cut labour forces by up to 60%. Best result was a £2 million p.a. saving.

- Successfully negotiated claim for contract cancellation, obtaining £1 million negotiated settlement.
- Controlled up to 500 staff through 2 reporting GM's. Responsible for £30 million sales and £1 million capex. Strong financial grip, including forecasting monthly profit and cash flows.
- Over 10 years' experience in corporate restructuring, including negotiating with Merchant Bankers Ing for successful sale of Stathern Electronics for £12 million; changing working practices, downsizing, introducing structured training, project management, MRP, TQM, ISO 900 into 3 companies.
- Technical background includes aircraft flying controls, propellant tanks for satellites, precision cable-handling machinery, sheet metal pressings and fabrications, heat transfer analysis, finite element stress and vibration analysis, fatigue and creep analysis, electronic and hydro mechanical fuel controls, aero engines and turbines.
- Strategic acquisition and management of IT mainframe and PC network systems, working with sophisticated CAD software and MRP systems, including Matra-Euclid, Pro-Engineer, Honeywell-Bull and IBM.

CAREER SUMMARY

2001–05 Managing Director, Stathern Electronics.
1998–2001 Managing Director, Stathern Systems.
1994–98 Director of Business Development, Stathern Group.
1988–94 Technical Manager, then Product Assurance Manager, Stathern Power Systems.
1984–88 Senior Design manager, Internal Electronics, (USA).
1980–84 Design Engineer, Rolls Royce, UK.
Age 46

FRANKLIN DONALD

Crowber Farm, Crowber, Sussex, SU 27 4BJ Telephone: 01556 987654
(Mobile) 01156 332 211

Fluent French, Spanish, Italian, commercial German – Divisional Managing Director in one of the world's largest multi-national groups. Controlled 21 companies in 16 companies in Ranching, Abattoirs, Hides, Skins, Leathers and Textiles; Fisheries, canned and refrigerated Meat manufacturing, distribution and warehousing; FMCG groceries; Commercial and aviation catering.

Experienced strategist and motivator of teams of international GM's. Broad international board experience.

Deep grasp of international trading practices, including setting up and closing down companies, plants, trading agreements, joint ventures, distributorships and agencies. Strong in financial monitoring, currency management, control of multi-national subsidiaries. Over 15 years overseas domicile – Europe, Asia, South America and Australia.

KEY CAREER BACKGROUND

- Consistent hands-on management experience of UK and international trading companies from £5 million to £200 million, labour forces from 30 to 1,000.
- Extensive corporate rescue experience, where closures, restructuring, return to profit and sale of 23 companies have been achieved. Transformed divisional profits in N. America, Europe and Asia Pacific from £265K to £8.8 million in 30 months. Led recovery of world's largest quality rainwear manufacturer from £3.4 million loss to £1.1 million profit in 2 years. Repositioned 5 disparate companies and sold them for £8 million over best expectations.
- International contacts in the Americas, Europe, and the Middle east. 10 years of specialised experience in Asia Pacific, including leading exploratory/development teams in China and Japan.
- Familiar with leading customer/supplier groups, including Sainsbury, Morrison, Asda. New Zealand Dairy Board, St.Ivel, Gerber, McCain, Sun Valley, Hershey, Borden, China National Cereal Board, etc.

CAREER SUMMARY

2000–05 Ranchester plc., Divisional Managing Director.
1995–2000 Ranchester – Regional General Manager, Asia Pacific.
1989–95 Ranch Tanneries – Group General Manager
1969–1989 Ranchester – joined as salesman, promoted through international roles to Managing Directorships in Argentina, Australia, France, Italy and Hong Kong
Age 56

Keep your CV right

Your CV is a personal sales document, so it will be different from any of the above examples. But there is a pattern, which becomes obvious as you read them. The emphasis has to be on **achievements** – not what your title was, but **what difference you made.** From this the reader gets a picture of how you might **benefit** his business – and that is 90% of the sales process.

As a matter of commonsense and good housekeeping, you should update your CV after every assignment, and send the update, usually by e-mail or on a floppy to each significant contact and Interim Service Provider. This serves to remind them that you are active and successful. In foreign parts, don't be shy – send them postcards! Just as importantly, bear in mind that 'searches by word' are increasingly common. So that latest assignment may include just the word that is driving a current search . . .

VII The professional touch

Avoid DIY – pay the piper (and call the tune)

Independents are by nature addicted to self-help, and when you're starting out the temptation is always to 'save the cash' when considering seeking professional advice. Our recommendation is; DON'T DO THAT! We've met interims who've lost thousands through not getting best advice at the outset. Think of the cost as a vital capital investment in your future. If you don't think your future is worth the investment, why are you reading this book? It is a complex, dangerous world out there – so get some professional armour!

Start with the bank

Bank managers – especially branches with a substantial commercial client base – can be useful friends. Be optimistic and positive, but be especially cautious in forecasts of future income, (he'll keep a file note of what you say). Bear in mind that, in this instance, you are not paying!

Here's a suggested Agenda for that important first meeting:

1. *Survival.* Show him your contingency plan for 6–12 months' survival without income, i.e. minimum-spend financial viability. Ask for his input.
2. *Business Plan.* Describe your Niche, with your draft CV. Explain how you intend to get business, daily rates, monthly targets.
3. *NETWORK. (a) For Professionals* – ask him to recommend an accountant, a pension/investment advisor, an insurance broker, a *commercial* solicitor. You can say 'thank you', and make your own mind up later.
4. *NETWORK (b) For real* – bank executives, especially in suburban/ provincial branches, get involved of necessity in many local activities – commercial investments and developments, job-creation schemes, corporate rescues, grant-aid applications, Chambers of Commerce, and so on. ASK his advice about who might be worth talking to next, who might have a use for your skills either for consultancy or Interim Management. Follow up that advice.

Your accountant

Could be your passport to that Big Rock-Candy Mountain where all your invoices are paid on time, and where the Inland Revenue's bite is rubber-toothed! Seriously, you need to be aware that most of his cost/time arises up front, when he is setting up your financial plan and tax plan. After that his annual fees will probably remain the same, but his costs should be much less.

Once again, it saves time/money if you go to meet him with a draft Agenda:

1. *Financial Health Check.* Be totally open and frank. Take with you notes of assets, income and outgoings. Many accountants also earn commissions as investment advisers. You might agree that such commissions should be rebated, and you will pay a fee for time/advice. He requires a 'full and frank' understanding of your circumstances in order to be able to offer best advice.
2. *Business Plan.* Take him over the ground, adding the bank's comments as appropriate.
3. *Legal Status.* One of the more problematic issues. As an independent freelance you could have a choice:
   (a) Self-employed sole trader
   (b) Partnership
   (c) Employee of your own limited company.

Most people start as sole traders, then graduate quickly to having their own limited company. Often the trigger is the first serious contact with an Interim Service Provider. Some will not even register you without limited company status; none is likely to accept an invoice from you without it. It is very easy and cheap to buy a 'clean' (untraded) limited company off the shelf, and the threshold before you have to have audited accounts is now very high. So you might as well 'get limited' at the outset. Your objectives in choosing your status are:

   (i)   To be as flexible as possible
   (ii) To minimise tax
   (iii) To maximise credibility with clients
   (iv) To stay legal

Make sure your accountant understands IR35, (i.e. suggest he explains it to you!) **Consultants** obviously do not fit the Inland Revenue's criteria for being classified as employees. But **Interim Managers** certainly could. By all the tests the IR applies, an Interim Manager could be a temporary employee, and, *irrespective of your assertion of* *'self-employed' status*, the IR could require the client to pay you through his payroll as an employee, with all the incumbent immediate deductions and extra costs to him for Employer's National Insurance. On the other hand, if your limited company is issuing an invoice for your services, and paying you a 'market-rate' salary less proper deductions as its employee, you have the beginnings of a case to argue, if necessary. **Take advice carefully on this subject – if it goes wrong it can be painfully damaging**. The administration involved in running a payroll with tax and National Insurance deductions for, say, yourself and your wife/husband/partner is quite small.

(d) *Fees.* Don't be shy – ASK. And negotiate if necessary. Ask for his hourly rate, and ask for a quotation for your first year. If you've come to him as a result of the bank recommendation, he won't want you complaining about the cost, will he? (Bad for future business!) Typically his annual fee will come to one or two days of your daily rate – and he should save you several multiples of that in tax alone.

Pensions/Investment adviser

You might be sufficiently impressed to chose your accountant for this vital function, but do talk to several before you decide. Initial chats are free. Typical issues include:

(a) *Pension(s) from previous employment* – if you have not already triggered this, do you know your exact entitlements? (Ask, and *get it on paper.*) What happens if you postpone starting for 5 years, say? What is the current Transfer Value? What would that yield in a fund of your choosing? (Make sure you are comparing apples with apples.) Could you access a useful Tax-Free lump sum?
(b) *Personal Pension Fund* – currently this is still one of the best ways to reduce tax, provided of course you generate income. Make sure the one you choose to receive your payments offers *total flexibility without penalty* over when and how much you will pay in, and when and where you can draw benefits eventually.

Insurance broker

It is *essential* that you carry Professional Indemnity Insurance. Every Interim Service Provider will require it, but it would be foolish too to take a direct contract without the security of insurance. You might build a 'hold harmless' clause into your standard contract – but every astute client will strike it out anyway, and what do you do then? Unless you expect to have your fingers on some very expensive buttons, Indemnity Insurance is likely to cost about one day's fee. If you wonder what protection you might get for your money, ask the broker to tell you some tales from his files – could give you a few sleepless nights though! Think what it might cost you if you have to go to the High Court to defend your company for a professional mistake you made. We recomment a minimum of £250,000 and half a million may only cost a little more.

Commercial solicitor

Probably the least of your worries. You will need to prepare a draft contract for any direct assignment, (an Interim Service Provider, when acting as your intermediary, will impose its own contracts on both you and the client.). Bear in mind this needs to be simple, so that a client can accept it, preferably without needing to run it through a corporate legal department.

Your limited company will come with a fairly standard set of company activities – it's not difficult to have these changed, and to change the name for instance, and these are matters a good commercial solicitor can handle for you. Ask what the costs will be, in advance. Do not use an ordinary family 'wills and conveyancing' solicitor.

A good practice with all professional dealings is to ask for a 'marker' – i.e. that you should be informed every time you are coming to a spend of say £300.

Outplacement counsellor

'Outplacement' is career-counselling advice for people who are being 'outplaced' – i.e. made redundant. Mostly this valuable service is paid for by the ex-employer. It can be a very personal service, so take time, if you are allowed, to meet several outplacement agencies, and take advice too from the company Personnel manager involved. If it's been five or more years since you were in the market to find work, outplacement advice *could* be very important, and worthwhile, even if you have to pay for it yourself. Outplacement Agencies can offer a whole raft of different services – you do not have to buy the whole package! Get competitive quotes for the three most useful services:

Psychometric
Constructing a CV
TV-recorded practice at interviews

Check that the agency is a member of a recognised professional body, and ask for a copy of their code of practice.

Index